Self-Management Therapy for Borderline Personality Disorder

Michael H. Langley, PhD, is a licensed psychologist and provider of employee assistance program services in Atlanta, Georgia. He received his BS, MS, and PhD from Purdue University. His current private practice is almost exclusively with outpatients diagnosed with borderline personality disorder. Dr. Langley also conducts workshops for professional mental health clinicians in self-management therapy with borderline clients.

Self-Management Therapy for

Borderline

Personality

Disorder

A Therapist-Guided Approach

MICHAEL H. LANGLEY, PhD

Springer Publishing Company
New York

Springer Publishing Company, Inc.
536 Broadway
New York, NY   10012-3955

94 95 96 97 98 / 5 4 3 2 1

Library of Congress Cataloging-in-Publication Data

Langley, Michael H.
  Self-management therapy for borderline personality disorder:
A therapist-guided approach / Michael H. Langley.
     p. cm.
  Includes bibliographical references and index.
  ISBN 0-8261-8300-X
  1. Borderline personality disorder—Treatment. 2. Self-
management (Psychology) I. Title. II. Title: Self management
therapy for borderline personality disorder.
  [DNLM: 1. Borderline Personality Disorder—therapy.
2. Psychotherapy—methods. 3. Self
Care. WM 190 L283s 1994]
RC569.5.B67L36   1994
616.85′8520651—dc20
DNLM/DLC
for Library of Congress   93-34856
                                                              CIP

Printed in the United States of America

This book is dedicated to the hundreds of enjoyable clients with a BPD diagnosis with whom I have worked. Their courage in facing unpleasant realities about themselves was a major force propelling me to write this book. I also dedicate this book to my three sons—Nicholas Martin, Neil Anthony, and Joel Patrick—and to my blended family son and daughter—Carrick Gray and Jennifer Van.

Contents

Acknowledgments

There are some short-term and long-term acknowledgments in order. My fondest acknowledgment goes to my wife, Jane Mollenkamp Langley. Her unfailing support and enthusiastic marketing of the manuscript was invaluable. Jane's reading of early drafts served both to sharpen my thinking and to help me realize that the manuscript, one day, would see the light of publication. I also must thank my little sister, Mary Jo Fitzsimmons, who always has believed in me and who gave me my first experience in unconditional love.

In addition to professional courtesy, heartfelt gratitude compels me to acknowledge certain medical people who "kept me alive" while I was writing the book: To Dr. Robert Lund, Dr. William Waters, IV, Chris Craig, and Cathy Kuharcik, I say "thank you" from a very difficult patient. Lastly, I want to thank my typists, Gail Faulkner and Pat Kalb, for their timely and accurate work.

Introduction

Borderline personality disorder (BPD) has proven to be a vexing psychological disorder to treat. Virtually every mental health clinician has a story about a "borderline client" that includes themes of long, tumultuous, and draining psychotherapy experience. Perhaps no other class of psychotherapy clients has such a negative reputation with mental health clinicians as do clients with BPD.

The psychiatric history of treating BPD is an inglorious one. Shaped by the principles and practices of psychoanalysis, the very term "borderline" originated to describe a class of patients who got worse, or were likely to get worse, undergoing psychoanalysis (Stern, 1938). In fact, it was not unusual for psychoanalysts in the 1930s through the mid-1960s to reach a diagnosis of borderline with a client because the client got *worse* while in psychoanalytic treatment (Kreisman & Straus, 1989).

The psychoanalytic therapy roots of the "borderline" concept have led to a legacy of extended treatment in which the primary focus has been to foster intrapsychic development. Largely through the use of therapists' interpretation and transference forces, borderline clients were "reparented" by their therapists. Therapy with this goal could last between 4 and 10 years (Kreisman & Straus, 1989). The success of this expensive and protracted therapy has been dubious at best.

The major reason for psychotherapy being unsuccessful with borderline clients appears to be the premature termination of therapy (Skodol, Buckley, & Charles, 1983; Waldinger & Gunderson, 1984). Serious questions must be raised as to whether client characteristics are the best explanation for why the majority of borderline clients stop their own therapy. Is it possible there might be an inherent flaw in either the process or content of traditional psychotherapy with borderline clients that makes the therapy inappropriate to their needs?

The self-management therapy model for treating borderline clients that is described in this book breaks fundamentally from most of the explicit psychoanalytic assumptions that shape psychotherapy for borderline clients. However, some of the core conceptual model of psychoanalysis—the presence of developmental damage during the first 5 years of life—is retained but integrated with other possible causative factors. Thus, the self-management therapy model conceptualizes BPD as a combination of developmental and trauma-induced self-disabilities. The self-disabilities produce the psychological, interpersonal, and lifestyle instabilities that make BPD such a painful and disruptive disorder. Rather than place the therapeutic focus on intrapsychic development and reparenting experiences through the transference dimension of the therapeutic relationship, the focus of self-management therapy is on borderline clients' interactions with their current environment.

A definitive part of being borderline is living in the midst of perceived psychological vulnerability, considerable chaos, conflict, and repetitive failures in living experiences. Departing from the traditional psychoanalytic focus on the therapeutic relationship, self-management therapy with borderline clients focuses on how these clients live outside of psychotherapy. Too much stress in therapy, regardless if the stress is psychogenic, iatrogenic, or sociogenic in its origin, will derail psychotherapy with borderline clients. Therapy should focus on helping clients manage the stress in their daily lives, regardless of its source. Traditional psychotherapy itself with borderline clients seems to be a major source of stress.

Self-management therapy essentially works from the outside in or from lifestyle issues into self, cognitive, and emotional issues. As will be noted, most borderline clients are dual diagnosed. That is, in addition to their BPD diagnosis there is an accompanying diagnosis of another personality disorder, an affective disorder such as anxiety, panic, or dysthymia, or an addictive disorder associated with alcohol, drugs, eating, spending, etc. Self-management therapy requires the clinician to be open and flexible to multiple therapeutic modalities—talk therapy, psychopharmacology, twelve-step and the self-help "anonymous" group activities, short-term inpatient stabilization—that are appropriate at different times to help borderline clients achieve and sustain adequate functional stability in their daily lives and relationships.

Until the 1980s, knowledge of the prevalence of BPD was based on little more than educated clinical guesses. Research data estimating the prevalence of BPD in outpatient and inpatient psychiatric populations are now much more available than is general epidemiological data about BPD.

Widiger and Rogers (1989) reviewed eight studies conducted in the 1980s that allow estimates of BPD in psychiatric populations. Three of the studies included 976 outpatients and five studies included 421 inpatients. Their major conclusions about the prevalence of BPD in psychiatric populations are as follows:

> The most prevalent [personality disorder] is borderline personality disorder, both in inpatient and outpatient settings. Prevalence rates for borderline have varied substantially across studies, but the best estimate based on all available studies is . . . 8% of all outpatients, 15% of all inpatients, 27% of outpatients with a personality disorder, and 51% of inpatients with a personality disorder. (Widiger & Rogers, 1989, p. 133)

Epidemiological data on BPD in the general community is more sparse. Again quoting the Widiger and Rogers (1989, p. 133) article, they estimate the prevalence of BPD in the community to be 1% to 2% without a clear indication of how they reached these percentages. Using a population base of 191 million people 16 years of age and older, 2% of that figure represents 3.8 million people who may have BPD.

Skodol and Oldham (1991) note that estimates of BPD occurrence in the community range from a low of .2% to a high of 15%. Again, using the population base of 191 million people 16 years and older, the size of the BPD population in the United States may range between 380 thousand and 28.6 million people.

Swartz, Blazer, George, and Winfield (1990) conducted an epidemiological study of BPD. They interviewed 1541 adults, ages 19–55, in the Piedmont section of North Carolina. The sample was randomly selected. In their sample, 1.8% ($N = 24$) were diagnosed with BPD. However, their most interesting data pertain to the use of mental health services by adults diagnosed with BPD:

> Data on health service utilization indicate that borderline respondents present for specialty mental health services but are not overrepresented in the use of general medical services . . . A report from three [epidemiologic catchment area] sites indicates between 15.6% and 19.5% of individuals with a recent [personality] disorder have had a mental health visit in the past six months. Nearly 50% of [this study's] borderline group have had one or more visits. Thus, even when comparisons are made to relevant sociodemographic groups, the borderline group is overrepresented in mental health service utilization. (Swartz, et al., 1990, p. 267)

It is becoming increasingly clear that BPD is not an insignificantly occurring psychological disorder. It is also likely that BPD is a significant financial factor in the nation's mental health bill. This latter point will become clearer in the next chapter when the data on BPD and co-occurring psychiatric diagnoses—the dual diagnosis issue—are presented.

This book is directed to mental health clinicians trained as psychiatrists, psychologists, marriage and family therapists, social workers, professional counselors, employee assistance program (EAP) counselors, addiction counselors, and pastoral counselors but who are neither trained in nor practicing psychoanalytic-type therapy. It is relevant to private practice settings, outpatient clinics, and inpatient facilities where borderline clients may appear for treatment. Its ultimate intention is to provide a cost-efficient model of therapy that will increase therapy successes with borderline clients while bringing down their therapeutic costs.

REFERENCES

Kreisman, J. J., & Straus, H. (1989). *I hate you—don't leave me.* Los Angeles: Price Stern Sloan.

Skodol, A., Buckley, P., & Charles, E. (1983). Is there a characteristic pattern to the treatment history of clinical outpatients with borderline personality? *Journal of Nervous & Mental Disorders, 171,* 405–410.

Skodol, A. E., & Oldham, J. M. (1991). Assessment and diagnosis of borderline personality disorder. *Hospital and Community Psychiatry, 42* (10), 1021–1028.

Stern, A. (1938). Psychoanalytic investigation and therapy in the borderline group of neuroses. *Psychoanalytic Quarterly, 7,* 467–489.

Swartz, M., Blazer, D., George, L., & Winfield, I. (1990). Estimating the prevalence of borderline personality disorder in the community. *Journal of Personality Disorders, 4* (3), 257–272.

Waldinger, R., & Gunderson, J. (1984). Completed psychotherapies with borderline patients. *American Journal of Psychotherapy, 38,* 190–202.

Widiger, T. A., & Rogers, J. H. (1989). Prevalence and comorbidity of personality disorders. *Psychiatric Annals, 19* (3), 132–136.

Background on Borderline Personality Disorder

1

HISTORICAL INFLUENCES SHAPING THE CONCEPT OF "BORDERLINE"

There are eight overarching themes that have shaped the evolution of the psychiatric handling of individuals with borderline personalities since the clinical recognition of this type of client occurred in 1938 (Stern, 1938). *First*, recognition of borderlines as a psychiatric group has evolved away from the schizophrenic end of the mental health continuum and toward the psychoneurotic end of that continuum. More specifically, the borderline condition increasingly is seen as a personality disorder with a heavy loading of affective or emotional problems. In fact, the current official psychiatric diagnostic manual, Diagnostic and Statistical Manual-III-R, has excluded all mention of psychosis or schizophrenic-like conditions as a diagnostic feature of the borderline personality (American Psychiatric Association, 1987). As a result, the diagnostic characteristic of "brief psychotic features" is no longer diagnostically relevant. A literature review by Gunderson, Zanarini, and Kisiel (1991) of studies of borderline clients revealed that approximately 75% report cognitive-perceptual dysfunctions such as depersonalization, paranoid experiences, and muddled or magical thinking. Nonetheless, the thinking disordered aspect of BPD, while very significant to therapy, is much less significant in reaching a diagnosis. As will be discussed later in this chapter, the minimum influence of disordered thinking in diagnosing BPD reflects the limited impact of the concept of dissociation on the current diagnostic features of BPD.

Second, the concept of "borderline" originated in traditional Freudian theoretical assumptions and classical, psychoanalytic, clinical practice. During the 1930s, 1940s, and even into the early 1950s psychoanalytic psychiatry held a virtual monopoly on how psychotherapy was conducted in the United States.

The "post-Freudian school of thought" is a phrase to cover a range of theorists commonly referred to as object relations (OR) theorists and whose influence in the United States was felt in the 1960s. OR therapy is typically traced from the work of the British psychoanalyst W.R.D. Fairbairn through the work of Margaret Mahler, Otto Kernberg, and Heinz Kohut. A major contribution of OR theories was to replace the Freudian instinct model with a psychosocial model of human development. It is OR theory that developed the concept of borderline pathology as narcissistic injury resulting from dysfunctions in the parent child relationship at a time when toddlers are 18–36 months of age. As Westen (1990) notes:

> Object-relations theorists reasoned that if psychosis is infantile and neurosis is oedipal, then severe character pathology (such as BPD) must be pre-oedipal, stemming from conflicts or deficits arising after the first year and before the fourth or fifth. (p. 663)

However, the findings from child development research have raised increasing questions about the relationship between BPD and parent-child dysfunctions during early childhood. Westen goes on to make the following points:

> If the assumption of a relation between infancy and psychosis (or psychotic levels of personality organization) is problematic, then there is little reason to suspect that the case is any different with respect to the equation of 'borderline' and 'pre-oedipal' ... developmental research suggests that children transcend many characteristically borderline and presumably 'pre-oedipal' phenomena—notably splitting, unambivalent and

noncomplex representations of self and others, and narcissistic or need-gratifying ways of relating to others—largely in the latency and early adolescent years not at the beginning of the oedipal period. (p. 664)

A final quote by Westen should make clear that a post-Freudian or OR conception of BPD is somewhere between fatally simplified and outright inaccurate:

> . . . I will focus instead on a less known body of literature in developmental psychology, on social development from preschool through adolescence, and particularly on the development of social cognition, which even more seriously challenges theoretical beliefs taken as axiomatic by object relations theorists. In short, what this research suggests is that our developmental timetables are seriously in error, and that many aspects of borderline object relations, such as splitting and minimal cohesion and maturity of representations, cannot be reducible to pre-oedipal functioning because they most resemble what is normal in latency and early adolescence, not in the pre-oedipal years. (p. 667)

It now seems clear that while OR thought has contributed many rich theories about BPD, an OR understanding of BPD is incomplete, largely inaccurate when compared with child development research, and difficult to integrate with non-OR ideas on BPD for a broader and more clinically relevant understanding of the disorder.

Third, since the 1930s and 1940s the central meaning in being borderline has changed from being untreatable (i.e., not able to be psychoanalyzed through therapeutic-directed emotional regression) to having a relatively intractable disorder with no clearly effective treatment approach. With the dominance of OR theory, BPD has become closely associated with an early-in-life (before age 5) narcissistic (self) injury resulting from poorly sequenced parenting (Chessick, 1983). Despite growing research evidence to the contrary, the widespread occurrence of abuse-type trauma during the first 15 to 18 years of life has not broadened the dogmatic view of BPD developed by the various OR theorists.

Regardless of whether the clinical populations of borderline clients are inpatient or outpatient, research data support frequent incidents of physical or sexual abuse experiences (Kroll, 1988). Until recently, consistent with the Freudian perspective, OR theories have tended to treat client's reported incidents of sexual abuse in one of two ways. The reported incidents were viewed as transference phenomena, which were seen as a normal and valuable part of therapy. Such incidents, especially if the "fantasized" perpetrator was a parent, also might be interpreted as carryover distortions that are unresolved from the oedipal period of development. With either interpretation, incidents of sexual abuse often were interpreted by OR clinicians as artifacts of therapy and thus not considered a part of clients' existential experiences.

Because of the theoretical assumptions of OR, trauma-inducing experiences in childhood reported by clients in therapy were "normalized" by interpreting such experiences as the result of unresolved conflict with the parents. In this way actual childhood traumatic experiences were revised by OR clinicians to reflect either early childhood developmental deficit or a developmental fixation. Such a view reinforced the psychoanalytic perspective of BPD as a toddler-based, developmental disorder.

As noted earlier, OR theories are at serious variance with research-based knowledge of children's cognitive and social development. However, differences between a BPD model premised on "early object loss" and individuation-separation problems and trauma-induced BPD are even more obvious. Brier notes in a trauma-induced approach to BPD, most documented sexual abuse does not begin until ages 6–12 years and the offending parent is seldom the mother and most often the father (Brier, 1989). With a trauma-induced perspective the entire OR matrix is turned upside down. Rather than the traditional focus being on the mother–child relationship, the therapy focus changes to the father–child relationship. Such a shift is tantamount to depriving experts of their expertise.

Fourth, the prevailing attitude of professional mental health clinicians toward borderline clients seems to have changed from an inability to treat them to an ambivalence about treating them. The mental health clinicians I've known and heard speak tend to blame their borderline clients for problems encountered in psychotherapy. It has been my experience that one of the great social and professional bonding experiences between mental health clinicians is to make reference to their burdensome experiences with "a borderline client." I've met few mental health clinicians who acknowledged their own personality style or therapeutic approach as a possible barrier to working effectively with borderline clients.

No published research was located in which the therapist's interpersonal style was considered as a variable in the therapy process or outcome with borderline clients. In a literature review of different individual therapy approaches with borderline clients, Shea (1991) notes the lack of controlled outcome studies of any psychoanalytic treatments of BPD, any interpersonal treatment approaches, or any cognitive therapies. She did report outcome results from a behavioral therapy approach that produced reduced self-mutilation behavior and a lower therapy drop-out rate (Shea, 1991, p. 1036).

The image of borderline clients as likely therapy dropouts is an image largely based on borderline clients' experiences in psychoanalytic therapy. That this dropout image may be mostly an iatrogenic factor associated with one type of therapy (psychoanalytic) is an issue virtually not discussed in the literature. It should be noted that the therapy drop-out image attributed to borderline clients is associated with the longest, most intensive, and most expensive form of psychotherapy practiced in the United States—a form of therapy lacking research support after 50+ years of effort.

Fifth, due in part to the financing of mental health therapy, in part to the development of new schools of therapy, and in part to the advances in psychopharmacology, regular multiple therapy sessions for borderline clients during the week are now very rare. As early as 1953 psychoanalysis and the less intensive analytic psychotherapy were known to cause problems in borderline clients. In a frequently quoted article, Knight noted the inappropriateness and risk associated with psychoanalytic treatment of borderline clients:

> The ego of the borderline patient is a feeble and unreliable ally in therapy . . . if they are encouraged to free-associate in the relative isolation of recumbency on the analytic couch, the au-

tistic development is encouraged, and the necessary supportive factor of positive transference to an active, visible responding therapist is unavailable. . . . Psychoanalysis is, thus,
contraindicated for the great majority of borderline cases, at
least until after some months of successful analytic psychotherapy. (1953, p. 10)

However, later in the same article, Knight points out that
even modified, analytic therapy is risky for outpatient borderline clients:

This attempt [at improving social adaptation] will often require
considerably more therapeutic impact than can be provided in
an hour a day of modified analytic psychotherapy. Both the
motivation and the specific opportunities for alloplastic adap-
tation can be provided through group dynamics measures—
group discussions, group projects and initiative-stimulating
group and individual activities. In a comprehensive attempt at
providing such a setting in which to conduct the individual
psychotherapy of these cases, we have discovered that many
such patients can be carried on a voluntary basis and in an
open hospital facility, thus avoiding the encouragement toward
isolation, regression and inertia which closed hospital care
sometimes introduces. (p. 11)

So it appears that even with supplementary therapeutic and
social support, borderline clients have trouble with even the
mildest forms of analytic therapy.

Sixth, the real contribution of OR theories to the current
conception of BPD is to view BPD as a *self* disorder. The failure of these theories to free the onset of BPD from parentally
induced frustration to toddlers has crippled seriously these
theorists' contributions to a more empirically based model of
BPD. What is evident is that most borderline individuals lack
a clear inner picture of themselves. In addition, their selves
include boundaries that erode under conditions of stress or
under virtually any intense emotional experience. The ero-
sion of boundaries leads borderline individuals to split or to
merge as a result of being overwhelmed. It is largely through
the processes of splitting or merging that the interpersonal
relationships of borderline individuals become so chaotic.
However, what continues to be too little recognized by clini-

cians is that the great majority of borderline clients who seek mental health help have a dual diagnosis. Typically, the dual or second diagnosis is an affective disorder (depression, anxiety, panic conditions), substance addiction, or another personality disorder. Thus, if a client is diagnosed with both BPD and anxiety or panic disorder it is not possible to attribute premature termination in therapy to BPD. Avoidance is frequently a major dynamic in people with panic disorders. Thus, to consider only BPD as the reason the client terminated therapy is to feed a stereotype and to ignore broader, relevant facts in a dual-diagnosis population.

Jonas and Pope reviewed 15 studies conducted during the 1980s to assess the co-occurrence of BPD and affective disorders. They concluded that individuals with BPD frequently suffer from numerous depressive symptoms and often have a diagnosis of a concomitant affective disorder (1992, p. 150). Gunderson and Elliott reached essentially the same conclusions but stated them much more specifically:

> The available evidence suggests a 40%–60% overlap between major affective disorder and borderline personality disorder among hospitalized and clinic patients . . . existing data indicate an unexpectedly high concurrence of affective disorder with borderline personality disorder . . . (1985, pp. 278–279)

Dulit, Fyer, Haas, Sullivan, and Frances (1990) looked at the relationship between BPD and substance abuse for 137 inpatients diagnosed with BPD. They found that 67% of this sample admitted to at least one substance abuse problem and of these 92 inpatients, 67 (73%) reported polydrug abuse problems.

Considerable research and analytical attention has been given to how clearly BPD can be distinguished from other personality disorder diagnoses. Zanarini, Gunderson, Frankenburg, and Chauncey (1990) compared 120 diagnosed borderline clients with 103 clients diagnosed with other personality disorders. The authors looked at four classes of symptoms—affective, cognitive, impulsive, and interpersonal features—in contrasting borderline clients with other axis II diagnosed clients. The authors summarize their findings:

> Taken together, these results suggest that the diagnosis of bor-
> derline personality disorder has descriptive validity in that its
> clinical features can be clearly discriminated from other axis
> II disorders. They also suggest that borderline patients and pa-
> tients with other axis II disorders share many clinical features
> commonly thought to be indicative of borderline personality
> disorder. These findings have important implications given the
> propensity of many mental health professionals to label almost
> all affectively intense, impulsive and interpersonally difficult
> patients as borderline. (Zanarini et al., 1990, p. 166)

What now seems clear is that BPD is a recognizable clinical
diagnosis, although no single BPD feature is unique to BPD.
In addition, people diagnosed with BPD usually have an accompanying psychiatric or substance abuse diagnosis. At
least two authors have noted the tendency of mental health
professionals to label intense and stormy clients as "borderline" whether they are or not.

Seventh, "borderline" has evolved from being a diagnosis
in between schizophrenia and psychoneurosis to being an
identified diagnostic profile of its own. Reich (1992) provided
a summary of different types of clinical instruments—paper-
pencil questionnaires, structured interviews—used to assess
BPD. While these various instruments all seem to measure
some aspects of BPD, no one instrument measures it
comprehensively:

> In general, the agreements [between instruments] are low.
> Agreement improves in populations where more severely ill
> borderlines are studied . . . and appears to worsen with milder
> cases. Even in more severely ill cases the . . . agreement is at
> best mediocre. (Reich, 1992, p. 131)

Lewis and Harder (1991) used 30 borderline outpatients
and a comparison group of 30 outpatients with other diagnoses to assess how well different measures diagnose BPD. The
four measures used were Kernberg's Structural Interview, the
Diagnostic Interview for Borderline Personality Disorder, the
Borderline Syndrome Index, and the Millon Clinical Multiax-
ial Inventory. The first two measures are interview instruments and the second two measures are paper-pencil techniques. If only one measure can be used for assessing BPD,

these authors conclude that the Diagnostic Interview for Borderline Personality Disorder is probably the best instrument
of the four (Lewis & Harder, 1991, p. 335).

From a clinical perspective the overlap of BPD with other
psychiatric conditions seems less a diagnostic issue and more
a treatment issue. Because the vast majority of borderline clients (perhaps 75% at a minimum) qualify for a dual diagnosis, *supplemental* diagnosis rather than *differential* diagnosis
seems to be the significant issue. From a treatment perspective a multi-treatment model is essential in which psychoeducation, behavior therapy, cognitive therapy, psychopharmacology, self-help groups, and lifestyle changes are used in an
individualized treatment manner.

Eighth, until the late 1980s the concept of dissociation has
had virtually no impact on the clinical conception or treatment of BPD. During the first half of this century, mental
health in the United States was dominated by the psychoanalytic model. A dissociative model of psychopathology has
never been a major theoretical or clinical force (1989, pp. 4–5).
Repression was to the psychoanalytic model as dissociation
was to the dissociative model. Putnam noted:

> Dissociative psychopathology continued to be identified during
> the 1930's. . . . Repression, however, with its putative active uncon-
> scious defensive function was considered responsible for the ban-
> ishment of unacceptable ideas, affects, memories and impulses
> from conscious awareness and voluntary recall. This mechanism
> was central to Freud's idea of a dynamic unconscious . . . Many of
> the formulations of dissociative symptoms came to be based on
> Freudian dynamic concepts. (1989, p. 5)

With these eight themes as a background, this chapter continues with a review of the historical and clinical evolution of
the borderline concept in mental health practice in the United
States.

EARLY CONCEPT AND CLINICAL IMAGE OF
BORDERLINE

Psychoanalyst Adolph Stern is credited with first using the
term "borderline" in 1938 when he described some of his pa-

TABLE 1.1 Borderline Features Identified by Adolph Stern

1. Narcissism
2. Psychic bleeding
3. Inordinate hypersensitivity
4. Psychic and body rigidity—"The rigid personality."
5. Negative therapeutic reactions
6. What looks like constitutionally rooted feelings of inferiority, deeply embedded in the personality of the patient.
7. Masochism
8. What can be described as a state of deep organic insecurity or anxiety.
9. The use of projection mechanisms.
10. Difficulties in reality testing, particularly in personal relationships.

Reprinted from A. Stern, 1938, Psychoanalytic investigations and therapy in the borderline group of neuroses, *Psychoanalytic Quarterly, 1*, 467–489.

tients as suffering from narcissistic (emotional) malnutrition. Table 1.1 includes Stern's list of ten clinical symptoms of his borderline patients. The following quote from Stern's 1938 article, reprinted in Stone's *Essential Papers on Borderline Disorder's* (1986), on borderline clients' negative therapeutic reactions to psychoanalysis is enlightening:

> Such phenomena [negative therapeutic reactions] are regularly observed in this group of patients. One notes depression, readily aroused anger, discouragement and anxiousness as responses to any interpretation involving injury to self-esteem. . . . With these patients analytic therapy is like a surgical operation. The surgical operation is a necessary therapeutic measure, in itself traumatic but necessary.
>
> Care then must be exercised that the operative technique be adapted to the particular patient at that particular time and not to the illness. Good judgment based on clinical experience, is of inestimable value here. A negative therapeutic reaction is nevertheless inevitable; in some the reaction is extremely unfavorable and, cumulatively, may become dangerous; patients may develop depression, suicidal ideas or make suicidal attempts. In these negative therapeutic states the necessarily dependent attitudes are exaggerated, and the demands for pity, sympathy, affection and protection made on the analyst are ex-

tremely difficult to handle; the transference situation, complicated as it necessarily is, becomes even more so . . . The result
is an increased clinging to the analyst as a parental figure. (pp.
468, 472)

This quote stands today as an indictment against the early
psychoanalytic treatment of borderlines. It is easier, after
reading this quote by a leading psychoanalyst of the time, to
understand the subsequent prejudicial stereotyping and professional mismanagement of borderlines that is very likely to
occur in today's mental health treatment settings.

Until the late 1960s the clinical concepts and therapy techniques of American psychiatry were shaped almost exclusively by psychoanalysis. The term "borderline" arose from
psychoanalysts' unsuccessful attempts to get borderline clients to submit to psychoanalysis. In the late 1930s, when Dr.
Stern introduced the term "borderline," American psychiatry
operated within a very limited diagnostic framework. By and
large patients were diagnosed initially as psychoneurotic
(neurotic) or schizophrenic (psychotic). In classical psychoanalysis diagnosis and early treatment often were not distin-
guishable from each other. Consequently, it often took a "borderline explosion" in psychoanalytic treatment before
psychiatrists could diagnose their patients as borderline. In
essence, this aspect of diagnosis was a type of diagnosis by
treatment failure.

The psychotherapeutic techniques used by psychiatry in
the United States in the 1930s and 1940s were quite limited.
During this period clinical psychiatry had no professional or
conceptual competition in the area of psychotherapy. In fact,
psychoanalysis was clinical psychiatry. Clinical psychologists
were primarily psychometricians of intelligence, attitudes,
and aptitudes. Social workers were concerned mainly with organizing urban immigrants into self-help communities. As a
consequence the theories, techniques, and prescriptions by
Sigmund Freud for psychopathology were compelling and
without significant competition.

In the 1930s American psychiatry used only two forms of
psychotherapy—traditional psychoanalysis and watered-
down psychoanalysis, which was called psychoanalytic psy-

chotherapy. As a treatment form psychoanalysis relied upon an intense emotional therapeutic relationship to be effective. This therapeutic relationship, unlike virtually all social relationships, was highly imbalanced emotionally. Patients discussed very personal information while the psychoanalyst remained relatively unresponsive and emotionally detached from the patient. The emotional purpose of the therapeutic relationship was to facilitate the patient's emotional regression so as to re-enact with the therapist the original childhood emotional relationship with one or both of the patient's parents. This therapeutic regression and reenactment occurred through transference. The purpose of transference was to have an emotionally merged therapist/parent experience in therapy as the patient relived unresolved (usually intense and painful) feelings with one or both parents. To facilitate this process therapists had to keep their own personalities out of the therapy relationship. The intent of psychoanalysis was to break down ego (or self) boundaries for the purpose of releasing repressed childhood feelings that patients continued to re-experience in disguised and destructive ways in their adult lives.

Patients in psychoanalysis who were neither neurotic nor psychotic, but who did not have sufficiently strong egos to tolerate the stress associated with the emotional regression occurring through the transference phenomenon, were labeled "borderline." In its original usage "borderline" meant "borderline schizophrenic." Because of the psychotic regression that occurred with clients who were borderline, major modifications had to be made in their psychoanalytic treatment. The emotional intensity of the psychoanalytic experience was decreased for clients who were borderline (Chatham, 1989, pp. 333–341). In essence, psychoanalytic treatment for clients who are borderline is simply "watered-down."

In the psychoanalytic treatment community, and then in the broader mental health treatment community, the label "borderline" quickly came to have an overwhelmingly pejorative meaning. Psychoanalysts believe that in order to practice their craft they have to stay emotionally detached (the formal term is "technically neutral") from their patients. This therapeutic requirement sets up a "no win" clinical situation for both therapist and client. The therapist's training in technical neutrality deprives borderline clients of the here and now emotional support they need to understand and to integrate their developmental and traumatic pasts.

However, when borderline clients responded unfavorably to psychoanalytic treatment, psychoanalysts tended to blame their patients and not the therapeutic procedures. This tendency to "blame the victim" for disruptions in the psychoanalytic treatment of borderline clients was acknowledged as early as 1938. Stern noted:

> Because these patients [borderlines] are gravely ill and because work on the transference relationship, acting as a frustrating agent, is borne badly by these patients, greater attention to supportive therapy marks one modification of technique [i.e., of psychoanalysis]. . . . The affectively immature attitudes, which manifest themselves for long periods and in great quantities, make intelligent work impossible, except for that which the analyst can . . . force the patient's healthy ego to accomplish in the understanding of this dependent attitude incident to his narcissistic needs. (1938, p. 478)

People were labeled psychiatrically as "borderline" because they were not treatable by "intelligent means." The cascading effect of an inappropriate therapy technology that clinically labeled an entire class of patients was now in place. What, in fact, was an iatrogenic failure (an inadequacy of the therapy), was projected by therapists to be a psychogenic problem within borderline patients. This "fact" became sociogenic as therapists began swapping stories of disrupted or counterproductive therapy with their borderline clients. Thus was born and perpetrated the stereotype and legend of the "difficult borderline client."

Both the psychoanalytic theory and therapy of borderlines was seriously incomplete. The borderline condition was seen as a developmental deficit arising from inadequate or harmful mothering. If trauma (emotional, physical, and/or sexual) is added as a contributing factor to creating borderline conditions, then the whole concept of a psychoanalytic approach to treating such conditions must be rethought.

The psychoanalytic therapy approach to borderline clients

was fundamentally inappropriate for two reasons. One, the approach requires an intense, one-way emotional relationship for the client. The client assumes all of the emotional risk and must generate most of the emotional energy in the relationship. For people with a borderline condition, abandonment and engulfment are the two greatest relationship risks. Unfortunately, abandonment and engulfment are two direct byproducts of technical neutrality and transference—two core therapeutic forces in a psychoanalytic treatment relationship. Traditional psychoanalysis fit tragically into the split in the struggle between abandonment and engulfment issues so central to the borderline condition.

Second, the focus of therapy on the therapeutic relationship rather than on lifestyle issues (work, relationships, use of leisure time, etc.), required psychoanalysts to ignore therapy-threatening conditions that existed in borderline clients' lives. As a result psychoanalysis often fiddled (gave historical interpretations and clarifications of clients' self-destructive behaviors) while clients burned (became overwhelmed by their current emotions or circumstances).

It should come as no surprise that many psychoanalysts, as well as therapists in general, developed negative emotional reactions (countertransference) toward their borderline clients. The psychoanalyst Harold Searles wrote of therapists' reactions to borderline patients:

> Typically the treatment process itself, in work with these patients, becomes highly sexualized such that the patient reveals newly-experienced and fascinating borderline symptoms in a basically coquettish, seductive manner, while the enthralled therapist struggles to match this priceless material with brilliantly penetrating interpretations. Typically, too, the treatment process becomes laden with acted-in aggression. For instance, ... the therapist who develops formidable quantities of hatred toward the patient comes to feel for a time that the only effective 'outlet' for this hatred is to be found in seeing the patient suffer from persistent symptoms. (1979, pp. 512–513)

From the 1930s through the 1960s psychoanalysts treated borderline clients by attempting to increase their ego strengths. It was felt that by titrating emotional frustration within the therapeutic relationship, a stronger ego would be the outcome. With a stronger ego borderline clients would successfully modulate their instinctually based aggression and sexual impulses. "Self" was not included in the initial psychoanalytic formulations and therapies with borderline clients. Instead, the therapeutic focus was on developing ego coping skills. It was left to the object relations school of thought to introduce self as a significant formulation in the theory and therapy with borderline clients.

THE INFLUENCE OF OBJECT RELATIONS THEORY

By the late 1960s psychoanalysis was no longer the dominant force in either American psychiatry or psychology. The explosion of biopsychiatry—treating psychiatric illnesses with biochemical medications—was well underway (Wender & Klein, 1981). In psychology, behavior therapy, cognitive therapy, and the humanistic therapies (client-centered, Gestalt, transactional analysis) had long ago left behind the assumptions, theory, and therapy of psychoanalysis. The post-Freudian era had arrived. However, none of these alternatives to psychoanalytic theory and therapy showed any sustained interest in a theory or therapy for borderline clients.

It was during the 1960s that psychoanalytic psychiatry itself began to change. Ego psychology and self psychology really began to have an influence on American psychiatric theory. This post-Freudian influence was consolidated in a school of theory and therapy called Object Relations (OR) (Hamilton, 1991). Although still psychoanalytic in its exclusive focus on explaining personality development through irreversible experiences occurring during critical periods in childhood, OR nonetheless represented theoretical progress from traditional psychoanalytic thinking. OR supplanted Freud's concern with ego/id relations with a focus on self-development through interactions in the mother-child relationship. The emphasis moved from harnessing biological forces to understanding psychological and social psychological forces.

While there is no clear historical watershed, the theories about the borderline state, influenced by OR, changed significantly in the late 1960s and early 1970s. Perhaps the biggest conceptual change OR brought to the understanding of the borderline state was to remove the nondescript meaning of the term from being neither a neurosis nor a psychosis. The OR concept of borderline includes a definitive profile of how a borderline personality can develop and the specific personality techniques that are a part of the borderline personality. However, three important limitations about the OR model must be kept in mind. First, OR is simply a modern version of psychoanalysis. In this sense, OR's major objective is to explain how inner self and other psychological images develop in infants' and young childrens' minds. An allied objective is to explain how parent-child relationships shape a child's self, personality, and relationship style.

Second, although OR produced interesting insights into borderline clients' psychological functioning, borderline OR theory has made minimal contributions to more effective psychotherapy techniques with borderline clients. OR still champions transference-based therapy that attempts to change psychologically the selves of borderline clients through the emotional dynamics that occur between the therapist and client. As a therapeutic approach OR shows virtually no interest in helping borderline clients manage their daily lives and relationships. OR provides a more focused version of psychoanalytic theory of the borderline state because the OR theory is more focused on one developmental period and recognizes the role of psychological splitting that blocks the self from integrating "either-or" types of experiences. But OR therapists continue to take a disinterested stance in the daily problems bedeviling their borderline clients, except as they may be disrupting therapy.

Third, OR continues the psychoanalytic tradition of limiting borderline producing personality (and self) problems to the preschool years. This limitation is particularly detrimental in reference to higher functioning borderline clients. There is growing clinical evidence that many people with BPD have suffered severe damage to their selves during the period of 5–12 years of age. As Dr. Jerome Kroll (1988) noted, many borderline clients report incidents of sexual, physical, and emotional abuse in their primary and secondary school years. Dr. Kroll also observed that borderline clients frequently react in particular settings or relationships like individuals suffering from post-traumatic stress disorder (PTSD). PTSD occurs with individuals as a result of an emotionally intense experience traumatic enough to produce disruption or discontinuity in the self. A PTSD-type experience is beyond the emotional range of normal human experiences and often requires psychotherapy to alleviate its consequences.

Despite the conceptual limitations of OR therapy, it is not possible to understand today's concept of BPD without recognizing the theoretical contributions of OR. An article written in 1967 by psychoanalyst Dr. Otto Kernberg provides a good overview of OR's conceptual approach to the borderline state. Dr. Kernberg (1967, p. 644) identified psychological "splitting" as a central process in the development of a borderline personality organization. He defined splitting as "a certain lack of integration of the ego." Although splitting had been discussed as early as 1950 by the British School of Object Relations as a personality defense mechanism, it was not given significant theoretical or clinical significance in mental health in the United States until Kernberg's work. Kernberg provided a more specific meaning for the term and used it to provide a foundation for understanding the development of a borderline personality.

The following quote illustrates Kernberg's distinction between neurotic, psychotic, and borderline and provides the term "borderline" with its own unique characteristics:

> In an attempt to differentiate psychotic, borderline and neurotic patients, one might briefly say that psychotic patients have a severe lack of ego development, with mostly undifferentiated self and object images and concomitant lack of development of ego boundaries; borderline patients have a better integrated ego than psychotics, with differentiation between self and object images to a major extent and with the development of firm ego boundaries in all but the areas of close interpersonal involvement; they present typically, the syndrome of

identity diffusion; and neurotic patients present a strong ego, with complete separation between self and object images and concomitant delimitation of ego boundaries; they do not present the syndrome of identity diffusion. (Kernberg, 1967, p. 677)

What is readily apparent from this quote is the absence of any implication that borderline clients do not function well in therapy. The preceding quote reflects the professional evolution from a definition of "borderline" based upon individuals' responses to psychoanalytic therapy to a definition based upon their psychic structures.

Kernberg's theoretical work on the borderline personality organization represents a transition from traditional psychoanalytic thinking to more contemporary OR thinking. While Kernberg continues to ground his thinking in instinctual urges and biological drives, he has provided relevant and clinically supported descriptions of borderline psychology. For Kernberg, splitting is the central psychological feature in the functioning of a borderline personality. Kernberg considers splitting to be a primitive coping technique appropriately employed by infants and toddlers. It is through splitting that people encounter experiences (including themselves) as "all good" or "all bad." Kernberg's (1967, p. 673) explanation of splitting as the result of "primary (from infancy) aggression or aggression secondary to frustration" reflects his background as a traditional psychoanalyst. Kernberg sees three consequences of splitting on infants' coping styles. Positive and negative images, affects, and experiences are kept separated as if they are two unrelated sets of psychological events. A second consequence is that the splitting blocks the dialectical relationship (or the interpenetration of opposites) between positive and negative psychological events. It is the splitting of this dialectical relationship that blocks the normal development of psychological modulation and restraint in the infant. For Kernberg this compromised developmental state becomes the basis for the chaos, instability, and explosiveness in the borderline clients with whom he has worked.

Kernberg believes a third consequence of splitting on infants who later develop BPD is the under-development of guilt and the limited development of empathy. It appears that Kernberg believes splitting locks the infant in a permanent narcissistic stage of development. Due to the frustrations associated with this developmental blockage, the infant copes by becoming a "rageaholic" and projects his/her hostility onto others and onto the self.

Kernberg (1967, p. 675) describes the implications of splitting on the adaptive capacity of borderline individuals. For Kernberg the sustained use of splitting in infancy has a determining influence on the psychological and interpersonal styles of individuals who develop BPD. As previously noted Kernberg believes such people lack empathic skills and experience other people as distant. This latter feature seems to imply the problems with abandonment that are such a central feature of BPD. For Kernberg individuals with BPD really have no choice but to avoid emotionally deep relationships and to "get by" with distorted (all-or-none) perceptions of other people and superficial interpersonal relationships.

In a subsequent statement about emotional shallowness as a part of the borderline state, he provides insight into the absolute inappropriateness of a transference-based, relationship-focused psychoanalytic psychotherapy approach with borderlines:

> An additional reason for their (borderlines) emotional shallowness is the defensive effort to withdraw from too close an emotional involvement, which would bring about the danger of activation of their primitive defense operations, especially projective identification and the arousal of fears of attacks by the object [person] which is becoming important to them. Emotional shallowness also defends them from primitive idealization of the person and the related need to submit to and merge with such idealized people. (Kernberg, 1967, p. 675)

Clearly, any form of therapeutic treatment that blurs a borderline client's self-boundaries, as does psychoanalysis, is contraindicated, unless the therapy is conducted in an environment in which the borderline client can be allowed to stay in this emotionally overwhelming therapeutic relationship until some psychological equilibrium can be attained.

Kernberg's last "transition to a contemporary approach" in

describing the borderline state is his acknowledgement of the central aspect of a flawed self and flawed individual identity in borderline clients. Kernberg (1967, p. 677) talks of the chameleon-like quality in many borderline clients' adjustment to reality. Kernberg describes an "as-if" quality in the adjustment style of individuals with BPD. The quality he refers to is the "fake self" image that borderline individuals develop that compensates for the lack of a real integrated self. This false self also is an adjustment to seeing people as need-fulfilling versus need-frustrating. The lack of an integrated image of others (sometimes fulfilling and sometimes frustrating) often leads borderline individuals to relate to others on the basis of the quality of the latest experience or on their expectation of the next interaction. Again, Kernberg traces these characteristics to the splitting in infancy that distorts all subsequent psychological development and interpersonal relationships.

OR's great contribution to detailing the borderline state is also its great weakness. Primarily through the work of Mahler, Pine, and Bergman (1975) the developmental stages in infancy and the preschool years, thought to be when borderline personality disorder occurs, have been detailed. Mahler and all object relations theorists and clinicians believe BPD to be an early childhood disorder associated with problem parenting by the mother figure. In particular, BPD is thought to develop as a result of poor synchrony between parent and child that disrupts or blocks the young child's successful efforts at early separation and individuation from the mother figure. The real contribution of OR has been to provide a schema that describes how the self is structured, how it functions, and how certain personality defense mechanisms associated with BPD operate.

The great weaknesses of the OR theory of BPD are threefold. First, it presents BPD as a disorder of infancy and thus orients therapy around one developmental phase in the borderline client's life. Explicitly this bias focuses therapy on the client's past rather than on the here and now. Second, the OR model of BPD places the problem of BPD exclusively within the mother–child dyad. The BPD-inducing problem is viewed more as poor synchrony between mother–child rather than any form of intentionally inflicted trauma. Third, because OR

considers BPD as an exclusively developmental disorder, neither theory nor clinical practice focus on possible unresolved
(or perhaps previously unknown) emotional, physical, or sexual trauma to the child.

Today most mental health clinicians seem to accept the OR
model that BPD is a developmental disorder of infancy or
early childhood. Simultaneously, clinicians seem to accept
most of the countertransferential-based beliefs of the psychoanalysts that borderline clients are resistant therapy-disruptive clients. Still minimally recognized by the community of
mental health clinicians are the iatrogenic contributions of
therapy that derail the successful clinical management and
treatment of borderline clients.

This book provides a clinical model of BPD that is both more
consistent with the research knowledge about borderline personality disordered individuals and more comprehensive than
the "critical stage" OR theory of BPD. The model presented
here—called a self-management model of BPD—incorporates
psychogenic, iatrogenic, and sociogenic factors in a combined
causal and treatment model of BPD. The model's central premise is that BPD is primarily the result of systematic exogenous
trauma that occurs sometime before the eighteenth birthday.
Relegated to a minor role is the central OR premise that BPD is
the result of a stage specific disruption in infancy of mother–
child separation/individuation disorder. Self-management therapy focuses on helping clients with BPD to live more effective
contemporary lives. Because of the presence of post-traumatic
stress, borderline clients must be helped to integrate such experiences into their personalities. Such therapy has primarily an
action focus rather than an introspection focus.

This book addresses a serious logical error in the psychoanalytic use of the term "borderline." Psychoanalysts have
considered the "borderline" concept in clinical practice to be
a categorical term rather than a dimensional term. In other
words, clients were considered either "borderline" or "neurotic" or "psychotic." There was no differentiation made between "more or less" borderline, despite the fact that some
borderline clients had strong enough egos to endure traditional psychoanalysis while other clients did not have such
ego strength.

A significant amount of disagreement in the psychoanalytic literature is traceable to individuals, samples, and populations of borderline clients who were, to varying degrees, more or less borderline. Thus, any group of individuals diagnosed with BPD is going to show great heterogeneity with respect to symptoms. For example, a hospitalized group of borderline patients generally will show much more severe psychopathology and reactions to psychotherapy than will a group of borderline clients in outpatient therapy.

This dimensional versus categorical use of the term "borderline" has been handled only coincidentally in the Diagnostic and Statistical Manuals-III and III-R. These manuals allow for a modified use of a dimensional concept of "borderline." From a pool of eight characteristics, any five can be used to reach a diagnosis of BPD. Such an approach recognizes the wide range of characteristics that comprise BPD, but such a diagnostic formula does not allow for a "more serious"–"less serious" classification of borderline clients. Certainly some characteristics, such as addictive behaviors, parasuicidal (self-mutilation), or suicidal threats or gestures, are more serious than others such as affective instability or fears of real or imagined abandonment.

Clients with BPD can be gravely ill, as was noted in the quote by Harold Searles, or clients with BPD can be imminently successful in one or more phases of their lives. The mental health fields have been negligent in identifying what factors lead a person with BPD to lead a life with some success, happiness, and stability. The operating assumption in the mental health fields is to split "successful living" people and people with BPD into non-overlapping categories.

The dimensional concept of "borderline" used here allows for the following flexible perspective. BPD is not a steady state disorder. It appears to be activated or to stay dormant depending on the level of trauma or stress in the person's life. As a consequence, it is easy enough to miss the presence of BPD in the initial diagnostic work because the majority of clients diagnosed with BPD also have a dual diagnosis.

A curiosity in the literature on BPD is the preponderance of women diagnosed with the disorder. The explanation usually given is that males who may have BPD often are diagnosed as having an antisocial personality disorder. This explanation is inadequate because the diagnostic guidelines in the current diagnostic manual call for making a dual diagnosis—both BPD and antisocial personality disorder—if both disorders are present. It is more likely that iatrogenic factors within therapy are at work and that in some unknown way these contribute to clinicians being more prone to identify BPD in women than in men. Of course, it is possible that the experiences of women growing up in the United States are more subject to traumatic or BPD-inducing experiences than are men.

Another missing element in the current diagnostic profile of BPD is the absence of dissociation. As the DSM-III-R notes about dissociative disorders:

> The essential feature of these disorders is a disturbance or alteration in the normally integrative functions of identity, memory or consciousness. The disturbance or alteration may be sudden or gradual, and transient or chronic. (American Psychiatric Association, 1987, p. 269)

Despite the centrality of splitting in BPD and the high comorbidity of BPD with Multiple Personality Disorder, BPD is not considered to be a dissociative disorder (Putnam, 1989). Dissociative disorders, among other causative factors, are induced by traumatic experiences (Putnam, 1989, p. 7). At this point in the professional mental health community, BPD still is viewed as caused by parent–child problems during a particular developmental period in early childhood.

REFERENCES

American Psychiatric Association. (1987). *Diagnostic and statistical manual of mental disorders* (3rd edition-revised). Washington, DC: Author.

Brier, J. (1989). Therapy for adults molested as children: Beyond survival. New York: Springer Publishing Co.

Chatham, P. M. (1989). *Treatment of the borderline personality.* Northvale, NJ: Jason Aronson.

Chessick, R. D. (1983). *Intensive psychotherapy of the borderline patient.* Northvale, NJ: Jason Aronson.

Dulit, R. A., Fyer, M. R., Haas, G. L., Sullivan, T., & Frances, A. J. (1990). Substance use in borderline personality disorder. *American Journal of Psychiatry, 147* (8), 1002–1007.

Gunderson, J. G., & Elliott, G. R. (1985). The interface between borderline personality disorder and affective disorder. *American Journal of Psychiatry, 142* (3), 277–288.

Gunderson, J. G., Zanarini, M. C., & Kisiel, C. L. (1991). Borderline personality disorder: A review of data on DSM-III-R descriptions. *Journal of Personality Disorders, 5* (4), 340–352.

Hamilton, N. G. (1991). *Self and others: Object Relations Theory in practice.* Northvale, NJ: Jason Aronson.

Jonas, J. M., & Pope, H. G. (1992). Axis I comorbidity of borderline personality disorder: Clinical implications. In J. F. Clarkin, E. Marziali, & H. Munroe-Blum (Eds.), *Borderline personality disorder: Clinical and empirical perspectives* (pp. 149–160). New York: The Guilford Press.

Kernberg, O. (1967). Borderline personality organization. *Journal of the American Psychoanalytic Association, 15,* 641–685.

Knight, R. P. (1953). Borderline states. *Bulletin of Menninger Clinic, 17,* 1–12.

Kroll, J. (1988). *The challenge of the borderline patient.* New York: W. W. Norton.

Lewis, S. J., & Harder, D. W. (1991). A comparison of four measures to diagnose DSM-III-R borderline personality disorder in outpatients. *The Journal of Nervous and Mental Disease, 179* (6), 329–337.

Mahler, M., Pine, F., & Bergman, A. (1975). *The psychological birth of the human infant.* New York: Basic Books.

Putnam, F. W. (1989). *Diagnosis and treatment of multiple personality disorder.* New York: The Guilford Press.

Reich, J. (1992). Measurement of DSM-III and DSM-III-R borderline personality disorder. In J. F. Clarkin, E. Marziali, & H. Munroe-Blum (Eds.), *Borderline personality disorder: Clinical and empirical perspectives* (pp. 116–148). New York: The Guilford Press.

Searles, H. (1979). The countertransference with the borderline patient. In Michael H. Stone (Ed.),*Essential papers on borderline disorders*, (pp. 512-513). New York: New York University Press.

Shea, M. T. (1991). Standardized approaches to individual psychotherapy of patients with borderline personality disorder. *Hospital and Community Psychiatry, 42* (10), 1034–1038.

Stern, A. (1938). Psychoanalytic investigation and therapy in the borderline group of neuroses. *Psychoanalytic Quarterly, 7,* 467–489.

Stern, A. (1986). Psychoanalytic investigation and treatment in the borderline group of neuroses. In M. H. Stone (Ed.) *Essential Papers on Borderline Disorders* (pp. 54–73). New York: New York University Press.

Wender, P. H., & Klein, D. F. (1981). *Mind, mood & medicine.* New York: New American Library.

Westen, D. (1990). Towards a revised theory of borderline object relations: Contributions of empirical research. *International Journal of Psycho-Analysis, 71,* 667–693.

Zanarini, M. C., Gunderson, J. G., Frankenburg, F. R., & Chauncey, D. L. (1990). Discriminating borderline personality disorder from other axis II disorders. *American Journal of Psychiatry, 147* (2), 161–167.

Dimensions of Borderline Personality Disorder

2

The self-management model of BPD requires clinicians to have a clear understanding of the following six areas: how the self develops through self-object experience; how BPD impairs the self; the role of shame and splitting as the core pathogenesis of BPD; Post-traumatic Stress Disorder as a co-existing and usually unrecognized condition affecting the stability of functioning of people with BPD; a delineation of why the OR's critical stage theory of BPD is factually and clinically inadequate; and clinical indicators of BPD.

HOW THE SELF DEVELOPS THROUGH SELF-OBJECT EXPERIENCE

The most clinically understandable concept of the self is associated with the work of Heinz Kohut (1977). Kohut is recognized as the founder of self psychology, a post-Freudian version of psychoanalysis that developed mostly in the 1960s and 1970s (Wolf, 1988). In short, Kohut's theory attempts to explain the development of self out of self-object experiences.

The following are Kohut's descriptions of "self" and "selfobject":

Self . . . refers to the core of the personality, which is made up of various constituents that emerge into a coherent and endur-

33

ing configuration during the interplay of inherited and environmental factors with the child's experience of its earliest
selfobjects. . . . As a unit that endures over time, [the self] develops in the lawful gradual manner of psychological structure. Among its core attributes, the self is the center of initiative, recipient of impressions, and repository of that
individual's particular constellation of nuclear ambitions,
ideals, talents and skills. These motivate and permit it to function as a self-propelling, self-directed and self-sustaining unit,
which provides a central purpose to the personality and gives a
sense of meaning to the person's life. The patterns of ambitions, skills, and goals, the tension between them, the program
of action they create, and the resultant activities that shape the
individual's life are all experienced as continuous in space and
time and give the person a sense of selfhood as an independent
center of initiative and independent center of impressions.
(Wolf, 1988, p. 182)

The term "selfobject" is described:

Selfobject is . . . neither self nor object, but the *subjective* aspect of a self-sustaining function performed by a relationship
of self to objects who by their presence or activity evoke and
maintain the self and the experience of selfhood. As such, the
selfobject relationship refers to an intrapsychic experience and
does not describe the interpersonal relationship between the
self and other objects. (Wolf, 1988, p. 184)

Despite being a branch of psychoanalysis, self psychology
acknowledges that, "every human being requires age-appro-
priate selfobject experiences from infancy to the end of life"
(Wolf, 1988, p. 11). However, self psychology does not accept a
"critical stage" theory of self development. Self psychology
recognizes the selfobject function as central to the development and maintenance of the self throughout the lifespan.
Self development, via selfobject experiences, "is needed for
life, and because the form of these experiences changes age
appropriately, we can talk about a developmental line of
selfobject experiences" (Wolf, 1988, pp. 53–54). In essence, self
development occurs at all ages and stages of life. This perspective has crucial implications for understanding and treating BPD. Perhaps most significantly, self psychology recog-

nizes important selfobject experiences shaping the self that are not in the mother–child relationship. Such a recognition about self development allows for the possibility that self injury leading to BPD need not be restricted to selfobject experiences with the mothering figure, nor must such an injury or dysfunction occur during the 18- to 36=month period of life. The "when," "where," and "how" of BPD-inducing self injuries become the focus of clinical inquiry rather than a theoretical/ideological assumption.

All object relations theories describe the self as emerging gradually out of the psychological fusion of the infant–caregiver that characterizes the symbiotic phase of child development. This phase is thought to occur during the second to fifth month of the infant's life (Chatham, 1989, p. 167). It is probably during this phase that the infant develops regulatory splitting skills such as differentiating "out there" from inside him or herself. It is also during this phase that the infant begins to distinguish in a reliable way "feel good" from "feel bad" states. Due, in part, to the fused psychological state, infants consider caretakers as part of themselves while also associating the "feel good/feel bad" states with what the mother/infant does (Chatham, 1989).

During the symbiotic phase it is crucial that infants bond or attach with their caregiver. In so bonding, infants are then in a position to experience the nurturing and soothing that are the major tasks of the caregiver during this phase. It is presumably during this period that infants experience a period of need-meeting, unconditional love. The OR contention is that if infants do not get this type of love, or do not get it in sufficient amounts, they may spend a lifetime compensating for it.

In addition to the regulatory splitting that happens with the occurrence of "feel good/feel bad" states, two other dichotomous developments are thought to begin during the symbiotic phase. To use Masterson's terminology, which is discussed more fully in Chapter 4, the beginnings of self and other images develop within infants during this period. As Masterson notes, both the self and other images develop as: (1) split self and other images, with (2) each image split into an "all good" and an "all bad" portion, and with (3) each of the two portions quite separate from each other (Masterson, 1981). At this point these "all good/all bad" psychological experiences and traces are not organized in any meaningful way. They are, however, the precursors to what eventually will be the young child's self-identity. During the symbiotic phase infants have no self-identity. Depending on the adequacy of the symbiotic experience there will be a predominance of satisfying experiences over frustrating experiences. The satisfying experiences provide the initial traces for the positive self-identity that the infant will have, while the frustrating experiences serve as the initial traces for the negative self-identity that will develop. As noted above, initially two part self-identities are quite separate from each other. By age 6 or 7 these two part self-identities should integrate into a fairly unified, though simplistic, self-identity. Such a unified self-identity is an example of what object relations theory terms "object constancy."

If, for some reason, symbiotic experiences are excessively frustrating, infants are thought to cope by developing a "false self," which is an effort to extract more satisfying symbiotic experiences with the caretaker. The false self coping involves infants taking on attributes intended to please the mother, or to be less troublesome to the mother, in exchange for more satisfying symbiotic experiences. In short, false self coping is based on the needs of individuals rather than on their preferences.

According to Object Relations Theory, it is during the development phase of separation–individuation that the developmental injury occurs to the self that leads to BPD. It is presumably during this developmental phase that many of the self functions originate that are absent or lacking in adults with BPD. These functions include differentiation from others, setting boundaries, autonomy, and the beginning sense of self (Mahler, 1971).

Within the separation-individuation phase is the rapprochement subphase. This subphase of development is thought to occur from the 16th to the 25th month of the infant's life. The rapprochement crisis of this period involves the toddler's struggle with autonomy and nurturing from the caregiver. Chatham has described this crisis in the following terms:

The conflict of this subphase arises from the toddler's contradictory needs for help and their fear of engulfment. They need and
want help from an outside source, but because of the individuation
drive and ongoing consolidation of separateness, they do not want
too much close body contact with their mother, whereas at other
times [especially at night], they attempt to coerce it. (1989, p. 185)

The successful resolution of the rapproachement crisis
results in toddlers integrating their need for autonomy with
their need to be connected to their caregiver. Chatham (1989,
p. 188) notes four factors that contribute to a successful resolution of this crisis:

1. The mother's successful balancing of the children's
   need for both dependency and autonomy;
2. The acquisition of language, which enables the toddlers, by naming objects, to let the world know their
   needs.
3. Identification with a good-enough mother and father.
4. The use of play activities for mastery and expression of
   wishes and fantasies through symbolic play.

Based, then, upon Object Relations Theory, the developmental injuries to the self and to the ego have occurred by age
2 in toddlers who subsequently will become adults with a
BPD. These injuries include the self splitting or failing to integrate the positive and negative portions of experiences into an
integrated total experience. It is important to remember that
OR Theory may be good psychological child development theory (though there are differences of opinion on that evalua-
tion), but what this book hopes to make clear is that OR Theory is simply erroneous when attempting to explain how a
BPD occurs.

HOW BPD IMPAIRS THE SELF

Without showing allegiance or favoritism to one or the
other Object Relations theories, a composite description is
provided as to how BPD either impairs the self or reflects an
impaired self. As noted in the preceding section, the development of self and individuality is thought to originate from the

fused psychological state that comprises the symbiotic phase of growth for infants. In this stage whatever psychological experiences and meanings the infant has are the mother's and are shared by mother and infant.

The initial development of self can be understood to pass through three phases on two parallel tracks. One track begins with the fused state of symbiosis and progresses to differentiation between infant and caregiver with independence, to a limited degree, possible around age 3 or so, when the skills of locomotion and verbal communication exist. A second track of development also starts with the fused state of symbiosis, progresses to separateness, and is followed by integration. It is important to remember that the development of psychological independence and integration evolves throughout our lives and does not stop with adolescence. One has only to note the prevalence of codependency to realize that the developmental tasks of psychological independence and integration are lifelong tasks.

Setting aside what causes BPD, how it affects the self seems pretty clear. Individuals develop self through a series of experiences with other people in whom they trust and on whom they are dependent. Experiences that are repeated, that have a great deal of continuity, that are relatively reliable, that include the influence or input of the individual, and that are acceptable or understood by the individual, shape the integrated independence of the self. Experiences that are too intense or too unintelligible, that are too at variance with the individual's experience base, or that occur too inconsistently, can fragment or split the self. It is the continuity of experiences in time and place that leads to cohesion of the self. Trauma is a major way the structure of the self dissolves or fails to function. The self, which is the repository of psychological meaning and motivation, has its cohesion split. Splitting can be seen as a self-protective defensive reaction. Current psychological meanings and functions are protected through splitting from experiences or meanings that, for a variety of reasons, don't "fit" into the individual's current self meanings or functions, or that threaten some aspect of the individual's self.

The self comprises a series of opposites (eg. good/bad,

happy/sad, informal/unaware, active/passive, spontaneous/
obedient, etc). The interpenetration of these opposites is how
an integrated or "mature" self is structured. This type of self
structure allows for two self functions. First, the self can provide its own check and balance function as a way to ward off
extreme or "all-or-none" reactions. Second, the self can modulate its own responses so that a more selective response or
meaning has a chance to occur. Selves that are not integrated
or that lack the interpenetration of opposites are split. It is
this split condition that can produce impulsive behavior, all-
or-none responses, selective memories, and distorted meanings. It is the absence of successfully interpenetrating psychological opposites that can lead individuals with BPD to feel
abandoned when they separate from another person, even
though the other person still thinks of them or loves them.

The self, then, consists of psychological opposites. The cohesion of the self is produced by the dynamic tension that
arises from the interpenetration of opposites. Self cohesion
must be understood as a renewable, dynamic property of how
the self is organized. Without the presence of integrated or interpenetrated psychological opposites the self is "flat." A
"flat" self simply means that the self is unresponsive to, or is
distortedly responsive to, experiences. All psychological experiences consist of oppositional qualities. For example, the experience of expressing anger also requires the person to re-
strain him or herself while expressing anger. The
combination of anger expression and the suppression of anger is an example of interpenetrated opposites and an example of what the self must be able to incorporate.

Virtually all psychological experiences consist of a mix of
opposite qualities. For example, an experience can include
both happy and sad dimensions, fulfilling and frustrating dimensions, or difficult or easy dimensions. If a person's self
development has not advanced to the point that opposite
qualities of an experience cannot be processed by a self structured to integrate interpenetrated opposites, then such experiences must be split, simplified, or distorted. This consequence is one impact of BPD on the self.

Another impact of a split self is considerable instability of
the self. A split self has lost the dynamic tension or stability

that occurs with the check and balance that exists from the outward tension produced by psychological forces held in some degree of check by their opposite. It is energy from this inner tension that both activates and modulates self activities. BPD limits individuals to a view of themselves, their circumstances, and their futures that is distorted, oversimplified, and often lacking in nuances. A borderline self does not integrate the oppositional aspects of experience. Over time individuals with BPD recognize their inadequacy to process and to manage psychological events, or they construct denial barriers against such recognition. Either way, they become seriously out of step, or perhaps overwhelmed, by events or people around them who have more normally functioning selves.

Both research and clinical work with victims of Post-traumatic stress disorder (PTSD) indicate that the self and behavioral consequences of PTSD are very similar to BPD. In fact, reviewing the pathogenesis of a PTSD victim reads like a client with BPD who is in intensive psychoanalysis and has been overwhelmed by the treatment process.

The theoretical and clinical treatment of BPD is traceable directly to Freud. The theoretical and clinical treatment of PTSD is traceable directly to Janet. Although these two theoretical legacies have been split from each other, the shared clinical manifestations of the two nosological groups—BPD and PTSD—is probably significant. At this point, the apparent largest difference between individuals with BPD and individuals with PTSD may be the stimulus conditions that trigger each disorder. If non-age specific trauma is considered to be a part of the development of BPD, then the two disorders show an even greater degree of overlap.

SHAME AND SPLITTING AS CORE PATHOGENESES IN BPD

Historically the central pathogenic process in the borderline state has been thought to be a latent or a nonflorid set of psychotic processes (Hoch & Polantin, 1949). Beginning in the early 1940s and continuing today, unmodulated or intense aggression has been presented as the central emotion of the borderline state. Referring to the psychoanalytic literature of the 1930s, 1940s, 1950s, and 1960s Kernberg (1967, pp. 646, 666) has been a major proponent of unmetabolized aggression as a central feature of individuals with a borderline personality organization. Kernberg, and the many psychoanalytic writers sharing his belief, trace the aggression to oral conflicts in infant development. These aggression-producing conflicts are thought to occur in the pre-oedipal phase of development (during the first 3 years of life). Kernberg posits that the pathological intensity of the aggression with people who have a borderline personality organization may be due to a combination of biogenetic predispositions and greater than normal frustration experiences in the early years of the infant's life. It is important to remember that Kernberg's borderline personality organization is a much broader concept than is the DSM-III-R BPD concept.

The emphasis on aggression as the core emotion in the borderline state probably represents a mix of clinical experience and psychoanalytic orthodoxy. In fact, aggressive expressions in therapy are frequently iatrogenically produced. Such expressions, which often reach the intensity level of rage, are a defense against shame. The following description shows that shame, not aggression, is the core emotion of the borderline state.

Shame is the neglected emotion in psychoanalytic writing and therapy. As Morrison noted:

> . . . I want to note the relative absence of discussion of shame in psychoanalytic writings prior to 1971 (with Helen Block Lewis's epic book). Since that time, and particularly in the last decade, papers and books have begun to appear about shame. It is as though this long-neglected affect has finally been taken "out of the closet" by psychoanalytically informed writers and therapists, after its neglect during the dominance of drive/defense psychology in traditional psychoanalytic thought. . . . I believe that such a change is due to a broadening of psychoanalytic theory to include the study of narcissism and the self. (1989, pp. IX, X)

Although Helen Block Lewis (1971) is credited with introducing shame into the psychoanalytic paradigm, the most significant clinical work on shame has occurred outside psycho-analysis. The father of shame theory is Sylvan Tomkins (1963; 1982; 1987), who wrote during the 1960s, 1970s and 1980s. For this text primary reliance is on the work of Gershen Kaufman (1989) to show the role of shame in psychopathology. Kaufman's work stands roughly midway between the academic writings on shame by Tomkins and the popular writings by John Bradshaw (1988).

The question, "What is the basis of shame versus aggression as the core emotion of BPD?" warrants an answer because this assertion is one of the core aspects of the self management model of BPD. Kaufman notes that when disgust or dismay (two forms of shame) are magnified and turned against the self, in defense the individual splits off these painful shame affects. This splitting can be fairly permanent, can occur without the individual being aware of it, and creates a mild to severe dissociative state (1989, p. 147). Thus shame is the original, emotional basis for BPD. Kaufman goes on to describe the relationship between shame and rage (or aggression to use a psychoanalytic term):

> A second important factor in borderline development is *rage*, an inflation or magnification of anger affect. Borderline development typically is associated with damaged narcissism. This is shame. The overtly displayed rage is the shame-based individual's secondary reaction to shame that has become magnified to the point of intolerability. Other defending scripts have not developed to either guard the self or mask shame from view. (1989, p. 147; italics mine)

Thus the emotion of shame provides an explanation of why and how the self splits in BPD. Understanding the role of shame in the borderline state reveals the all too frequent aggressive expressions or demonstrations of rage vis-a-vis therapy and therapist as a defense against shame exposure rather than as an expression of a primary, borderline-related emotion of aggression.

It is important to differentiate healthy shame from toxic shame. Healthy shame is the reaction each of us has to our objective limitations. For example, objective limitations include the inability to defy gravity, to read another person's mind, to own all the property in town, to have everyone in our state know us. These personally limiting conditions create healthy shame and this type of shame is simply the result of limitations placed on us by objective circumstances. The failure to own all of the property in town is more the constraint of objective circumstances than it is a personal failure or inadequacy on the part of the individual. Healthy shame serves a regulatory or self protection function by helping to set a standard of what is possible, normal, or adequate.

The passage from healthy shame to toxic shame occurs when a limitation becomes an inadequacy or a condition of inferiority for the individual. Life is lived between the very broad parameters of perfectionism, total satisfaction, or unconditional acceptance and complete flawedness, abject misery, or total rejection. Healthy shame reflects our acceptance of our own objective limitations or flaws. Toxic shame seems to occur when we fail to meet an expectation or an ideal that we hold for ourselves. The healthy shame associated with not owning all the property in our home town, for example, becomes toxic shame if individuals hold an expectation or ideal for themselves to be a monopolistic property owner. Both healthy and toxic shame are forces integrally connected to the development of the self. The psychoanalytic concept of shame is that of an emotion that is both infantile and primitive and not particularly relevant developmentally. In this text shame is considered a vital force in the development and function of the self throughout the entire lifespan. Shame is a core part of all self disorders of which PBD is only one. In the next chapter a description of how shame develops will be provided.

Within the psychoanalytic ranks and the community of mental health clinicians in general, splitting has been recognized since the 1960s as a core coping process used by individuals with BPD. It was Kernberg who initially focused attention on the relationship between splitting and being borderline. Kernberg (1967, p. 667) saw the splitting process in infancy as either the core coping mechanism or the only coping mechanism borderline individuals have for containing their aggression. Kernberg seems to limit his use of the term "splitting" to its primitive occurrence in infancy and then to its recurrence in a form of "repetition compulsion" until the individual receives successful psychoanalytic therapy.

As will be shown later in this chapter, the psychoanalytic meaning of the term "splitting" is both restrictive and distorting. Only a few moments of introspection will reveal that each of us engages in various forms of splitting and such splitting is not necessarily primitive, defensive, or distorting. In fact, the very foundation of Aristotelian logic is premised on accurate and systematic splitting of reality into mutually exclusive and all-inclusive categories of thought, reality, and experience.

Splitting must be assessed clinically regarding its pathological function and components, rather than simply assuming the presence of pathology. Part of what makes BPD such a complex disorder is the unreliable mix of reality-based and reality-distortion splitting.

PTSD AS A PART OF BPD

Earlier in this chapter PTSD was mentioned as a faulty self-object experience. As will be shown in this section, shame and pathological splitting are central aspects of PTSD. All PTSD victims do not become borderline, but all individuals with BPD have unresolved PTSD in their background. In many instances the PTSD fails to meet prevailing diagnostic criteria. The unresolved trauma, nevertheless, must be dealt with clinically. PTSD produces temporary or permanent change in the victim's self-identity and daily functioning through the experiencing of extreme environmental events. These events are so extreme that a person's normal coping resources and identity-confirming behaviors are inadequate or inappropriate for coping with the situation.

In terms of psychiatric classification, PTSD is considered an anxiety disorder (Schwartz, 1990, p. 221). Anxiety, though, may not be the central pathogenic process occurring in PTSD. Many of the diagnostic characteristics in the DSM-III-R support a strong anxiety component in a PTSD (American Psychiatric Association, 1987). However, the briefest of clinical contact with a PTSD victim will reveal the central role played by shame in this disorder. PTSD occurs because an unusual experience happened that overwhelmed the individual. Stated another way, the individual is inadequate, inferior, insignificant, inept, or impotent in the situation that produced the PTSD. It is how the shame is handled, with the resultant impact on the self, that produces a PTSD. The anxiety aspect of PTSD that is highlighted in the DSM-III-R is simply a secondary reaction to bypassed shame.

With the diagnostic emphasis on anxiety-related features, it is easy to overlook two other significant features of PTSD. One of these features is dissociation, which leads to splitting as a central coping technique for managing the trauma. Depending on the health of the PTSD victim's personality structure, the characteristics of the trauma and the post-trauma response to the victim, the type and degree of splitting that occurs will vary. The concept of splitting, with its psychoanalytic origins, has been unduly restrictive with a meaning that is either a primitive psychological defense of infancy or indicative of a psychotic or near-psychotic psychiatric condition in adults (Langley, 1992). In fact, splitting seems to be a daily psychological technique for virtually every adult.

A second feature of PTSD is that it is a disorder of the self. Crucial in an experience that produces PTSD is the sense of helplessness and the loss of autonomy. Both of these psychological experiences can alter or collapse the victim's self structure. It is this assault on the self that produces the emotional damage of PTSD. The diagnostic focus is on the emotion of anxiety in PTSD but the core debilitating emotion of PTSD is shame. Portions of the victim's self structure collapse. Such a collapse has two immediate consequences for PTSD victims. First, such victims cease to function as they normally did prior to the traumatic event. For example, their autonomy, ability to initiate, willingness to be alone, or their eating and sleeping patterns become less effective or less efficient. Second, PTSD victims see themselves as less effective people. They may become acutely aware of their own mortality, or they may see themselves as flawed or undesirable. Successful treatment must address both of these aspects of PTSD. A question as yet unanswered concerns whether or not the failure to treat PTSD leads such a person to develop a BPD af-

ter a certain period of time or because of subsequent intervening experiences.

Schwartz describes a biopsychosocial treatment approach
to PTSD. In discussing the psychological therapies, Schwartz
identifies the following emotions that must be abreacted with
PTSD victims: fear, anger, survivor guilt, shame, and any positive feelings present during the trauma and anxiety. As Schwartz (1990, pp. 229–230) notes, "All of these cases would
stand little chance for improvement without eventual acknowledgement and working through of these feelings of
shame."

In a subsequent chapter the numerous dimensions and
manifestations of shame will be described. It is imperative in
developing a trauma-based understanding of BPD and how to
treat it to understand how shame affects the self, what the
shame-related defenses are, and specifically, the role of
shame in both PTSD and BPD.

At this time neither research, theory, nor clinical experience support the position that BPD is a form of chronic PTSD.
However, it is conceivable that this position could become de-
fensible as BPD formulations break free from their psychoanalytic moorings and more fully capture the psychic trauma
that seems so central to the borderline clients who seek mental health treatment. As Schwartz (1990, p. 223) reminds us,
we now know that PTSD can occur in either adulthood or
childhood. Until recently PTSD simply was considered an
adult disorder. Because the clinical concerns about PTSD involved soldiers who were traumatized in combat, the possibility of PTSD occurring in children simply was not addressed
until recently.

As van der Kolk, Brown, and van der Hart (1989, p. 366)
noted, "the central psychoanalytic tenet that most psychopathology is the result of a childhood intrapsychic conflict between unacknowledged instinctual drives and external reality
left little room for an integrated understanding of the emotional, cognitive and biological effects of human traumatization." Even with the post-Freudian thinking that gathered mo-
mentum in the 1960s and 1970s the emphasis, though much
more on social and psychological forces, still focused all major causes of psychopathology in childhood.

Until the 1980s a major cost of the hegemony of Freudian thought on mental health practices has been the invisibility of the work of the psychiatrist Pierre Janet. Janet considered dissociation as the main psychological process "in the genesis of a wide variety of post traumatic symptoms" (van der Kolk, et al., 1989, p. 366). The PTSD model that Janet developed at the turn of the 19th century continues largely intact today and has been surpassed by no other model.

According to van der Kolk, et al. (1989, p. 368) "Janet believed that traumatization resulted from failure to take effective action against a potential threat. The resulting helplessness gave rise to 'vehement emotions' which, in turn, interfered with proper memory storage." Janet recognized the heavy phenomenological basis of PTSD. He noted that the stimulus to PTSD need not be dramatic. Rather, "it is the intensity of the emotional *reaction* that determines whether an event precipitates post traumatic psychopathology (van der Kolk, et al., 1989, p. 375).

Janet offers three important bridges that help connect PTSD to BPD. One bridge is that a post traumatic stress reaction can develop from a *subjectively* traumatizing experience. The meaning, rather than an objective event or stimulus, is crucial in the occurrence of a post-trauma disorder. Thus, an objective observer (clinician) cannot ipso facto declare a certain kind of experience traumatic. The reaction of the participant (or client) is a requisite variable in assessing the presence or absence of trauma. Thus, neither separation nor individuation problems between toddlers 18 months to 36 months old and their mothers have inherent trauma built into them. Yet people can develop BPD even though the aforementioned mother-child "trauma" did not occur. In fact, this author questions whether a child 18–36 months of age is developed sufficiently to have PTSD. Furthermore, the unexpected, shock, or overwhelming dimension of the stimulus necessary to generate the subjective trauma needed for PTSD raises an interesting question. Is the failure of a mother to respond with mutual cuing to her toddler, or the mother frustrating this toddler's autonomy strivings, or not satisfying the toddler's need for nurturing a severe enough experience to produce trauma? The Object Relations Theory of BPD suggests that these experiences can be traumatic to the toddler. However, the shock quality and overwhelming nature that is a central part of a trauma experience does not seem to be a part of mother-child interactions that leave the child frustrated or unfulfilled.

The second bridge that links PTSD to BPD is that rarely does the traumatic response of a PTSD victim occur at the time of the stressed event. Trauma in two areas—separation and individuation—of a mother-toddler relationship clearly cannot be eliminated as playing a possible trauma role in BPD. However, it does not make sense to limit BPD-related trauma to one relationship in one phase of life. What has to be explained is the long lag time of many years between the occurrence of childcare-related trauma in early childhood and the manifestation of BPD 1 to 2 decades later. The separation by time of PTSD from its triggering event and subsequent BPD allows for three possibilities. First, the effects of the traumatic event(s) potentiated over time, gathering intensity in their dissociated "stuck" state. Second, once the child is traumatized and BPD begins developing, there is an accumulation of "major" or "minor" traumatic events in the growing-up years that eventually reaches the threshold of a psychiatric disorder. Third, a person living with dissociated trauma copes with it until he or she is ready to address the psychological pain.

The third bridge that connects PTSD and BPD is that both are disorders of the self and both employ a form of dissociation (splitting in terms of BPD). The two concepts—dissociation and splitting—differ more in their intellectual histories than they do in their applied clinical meaning. Dissociation is a term traceable to the work of Janet (Counts, 1990, p. 361). Splitting is a term traceable back through Melanie Klein to Freud (Hinsie, & Campbell, 1975, p. 713). In fact, Grotstein (1981) sees splitting as a direct result of dissociation or as one type of dissociation. Thus PTSD and BPD share dissociation as a major coping mechanism. As Counts (1990, p. 467) notes, "often mental health professionals use the term dissociation when they mean repression." Repression is a term with psychoanalytic origins. For consistency purposes, dissociation is probably the preferred term for showing the trauma connection between PTSD and BPD. Whether a client has only PTSD, BPD, or both, dissociation is employed to protect the self structure from trauma-induced vulnerability. It is important to remember that structure in the psychological sense means "pattern based upon repetition." Self structure results from consistent self-object experiences. The structure of the self can be broken temporarily or permanently by experiences significantly at variance with previous self-object meanings and which contain overwhelming levels of emotional intensity.

There is a fourth bridge that ties together PTSD and a trauma-based model of BPD. The core pathological emotion of both disorders is shame. Historically, some variation of blocked anxiety has been assumed to be the central emotion in PTSD.

> By its very nature, shame may be expected to be concealed or disguised. . . . The tearing of the fabric, the disruption, provides the setting and the occasion for what has come to be known as shame. In this and other ways, shame can and does play a significant role in every phase of the acquisition, manifestation and treatment of PTSD. (Stone, 1992, p. 133)

The "tearing of the fabric" to which Stone refers is a symbolic way of referring to the self-object structure shattered by a traumatic experience. A self structure can be shattered by an experience that is sufficiently overwhelming emotionally. The individual cannot then titrate its intensity so that the experience can be integrated into current structures of meaning. An experience also can shatter self structures by being so negatively novel or foreign in its meaning that there is no place for this experience to be incorporated into the self. However, its impact on the individual is too powerful to be denied or avoided so it gets split off from the existing self or psychological meaning structure and develops its own separate structure.

The discussion in this book begs the question of the initial causation of BPD. What it does try to make clear is how toxic shame seems to damage the self. This initial damage appears to occur through splitting which, from a psychoanalytic perspective splitting has been presented as occurring because of an excess or flooding condition. Splitting also can occur because of the "unnatural" separation of the interpenetrated opposites that comprise all psychological experiences. In other words, the numbing that can occur when a parent slaps a child in public is the role that shame may play in splitting off "hatred for the behavior" from "love of the person." Thus, splitting also can function to split opposite qualities that for reasons, for example, of intensity, frequency, or duration do not get integrated into the person's self system. Shame may lead to splitting as a way to preserve either a particular self or social image people have of themselves, or an image held of another person. Shame also can split attention, perception, memory, and attitude such that hesitancy or ambivalence is usually a central feature of a shame experience. Re-integration of the affected psychological function or a particular psychological experience becomes a major objective in clinical work with shame.

In BPD, historically unmetabolized or excessive aggression has been assumed to be the central emotion. In fact the excessive anger or rage of borderline clients are psychological defenses used to ward off awareness or detection of the debilitating presence of shame. Bradshaw has provided the following description of the relationship between excessive hostility (rage) and shame:

> Rage is probably the most naturally occurring cover-up for shame. . . . Although the rage, expressed as hostility or bitterness, was originally intended to protect the self against further experiences of shame, it becomes internalized also. Rage becomes a state of being, rather than a feeling among many other feelings. (1988, p. 90)

The clinical issue of shame becomes magnified with the confluence of shame from a traumatic experience and a characterological disorder. In the self-management model of BPD to be presented here, shame is identified as the core emotion of this disorder.

SHORTCOMINGS IN THE OR THEORY OF BPD

The preceding section provides an important context for re-examining BPD as a developmental disorder of early childhood. Kernberg's "borderline personality organization" is a much broader term than is DSM-III-R-based BPD. The former concept refers to a generalized level of personality development. As Westen notes:

> Although as a shorthand one may appropriately refer to a patient as organized at a particular overall level of functioning [borderline], 'object relations' is not a unitary phenomenon or developmental line. It is a broad rubric encompassing a large number of cognitive, affective and motivational processes that are interdependent but distinct in their functions and developmental trajectories. Patients may evidence pathology on some or all of these dimensions, and the covariation of different aspects of pathological functioning is an empirical question. No person functions at a single level of object relations all the time. (1990, p. 686)

The numerous manifestations of BPD suggest, on logical grounds, that individuals with BPD would mimic each other more closely in their symptoms than they do. As Kroll (1988, p. 8) has pointed out using the DSM-III-R diagnostic characteristics, there are 56 different variations of BPD.

Certainly the age that a trauma or developmental disruption occurs is a significant variable in subsequent psychopathology. However, it is not all-determining:

> Since object relations develop throughout childhood and adolescence, experiences that inhibit or alter development can affect enduring object-relational structures at any point. . . . The affective quality of the object world and the capacity to invest in other people are fundamentally shaped in the pre-oedipal years, so that disrupted or abusive attachments are highly pathogenic. The extent to which later experiences can create or prevent severe object-relational pathology and the factors that permit some children to develop the capacity for relatedness and a sense of interpersonal trust despite pathogenic pre-oedipal experiences are largely unknown. (Westen 1990, pp. 688-689)

Two significant points can be made from this quote. While experiences in the pre-oedipal period, when OR theory says developmental disruption leading to BPD occurs, may dictate the affective quality of a person's personality, the cognitive and motivational processes in that same personality are not so seriously affected. Consequently, at best, such a disruption is insufficient to account for the wide variations in BPD. Second, the impact of developmental disruptions later than the pre-oedipal years still remains unknown. Scientifically, it should be clear that a trauma-based model of BPD can coexist with an OR theory of BPD and, with continuing research, likely will override the OR theory of BPD.

The last point to be made on the limits of current OR theory is that many people with BPD never appear for mental health treatment, appear to live "good enough" lives and, in some instances, excel in one or more areas of their lives. OR theories of BPD seem to allow for no successful "compensatory" living where people with BPD develop lifestyles that allow for their disorder, get in adult relationships that are "good enough," and maintain sufficient structure that allows them adequate self-object experiences. Yet I would be surprised if every reader of this book did not know a person with BPD who lives "good enough" without the aid of psychotherapy.

BPD AND ADDICTIONS

According to the DSM-III-R, one of the diagnostic criteria for BPD is:

> . . . impulsiveness in at least two areas that are potentially self-damaging, e.g., spending, sex, substance abuse, shoplifting, reckless driving, binge eating. . . . (American Psychological Association, 1987, p. 347)

For numerous individuals with BPD their impulsive behavior develops a chronicity. Perhaps due to poor self-regulation, chronically impulsive behavior evolves into compulsive or addictive behavior. A significant number of individuals with BPD develop a dual diagnosis condition as they become addicted to some substance or some activity. The significance of this number is open to debate.

There are three frequently occurring sets of co-morbid psychiatric conditions with BPD. Affective disorders (primarily depression and anxiety and, to a lesser extent, panic disorders and obsessive-compulsive disorder), other axis II personality disorders (most frequently antisocial, histrionic, and passive personality disorders), and substance abuse (most frequently alcohol and sedative-hypnotics) co-occur most often with BPD (Gunderson & Elliott, 1985, p. 278; Skodol & Oldham, 1991, p. 1026; Dulit, Fyer, Haas, Sullivan, & Frances, 1990, pp. 1003–1004).

The heterogeneity of BPD causes research methodology problems, because this heterogeneity leads to non-comparable populations of individuals with BPD. As a result, generalizations about individuals with BPD and co-morbid diagnosis must be made carefully. Most fundamentally, BPD inpatient populations seem to differ from BPD outpatient populations. Second, BPD and a co-morbid diagnosis seem to interact and usually make for a poorer prognosis. A significant minority of individuals in treatment for BPD also have a problem with addiction. Likewise, a significant minority of individuals in treatment for an addiction have BPD.

The perspective advocated in self-management therapy is that active substance abuse or compulsive activity must stop if the person wants psychotherapeutic help. Stopping the compulsive drug use or activity usually can be accomplished through behavioral contracts, the use of significant others, family and social support, and the participation in a relevant self-help group. The clinician must be willing to tolerate relapses when working with such a dual diagnosis individual on an outpatient basis.

Little research exists on the treatment outcomes of populations with BPD and a dual addiction diagnosis. Such work is beginning to appear with eating disordered women who have BPD. Sansone and Fine (1992) conducted a 3-year follow-up study with 19 women being treated for an eating disorder. A dimensional, rather than either-or, measure of BPD was used. These authors found a consistent relationship between the extent of the borderline psychopathology and negative outcome of treatment. They noted:

> . . . borderline symptoms were related to greater emotional maladjustment and distress; less satisfaction with life; and, on some borderline measures, fewer perceived positive changes in

eating disorder symptomatology, [greater] use of psychotropic medication, and continued mental health treatment. (Sansone & Fine, 1992, p. 183)

Intuitively, having BPD would seem to increase the risk of sustaining a successful addiction recovery. The instabilities of self, cognition, emotion, and behavior—so much a part of BPD—would impede the routine, one-day-at-a-time pace that is so important to sustaining recovery. The interpersonal instability of BPD is likely to make difficult the development of appropriate relationships within a recovery community. Many people with BPD have difficulty balancing relationships between the poles of engulfment and isolation.

No research or analysis could be found in the literature that examined the experiences of a recovering person with BPD in one of the Anonymous self-help groups. Any clinician or treatment team working with a client with BPD who is going to join, for example, Alcoholics Anonymous (AA), should provide a good deal of structure and support during the entry period. It is so important for the clinician to be aware of any splitting that may occur between the therapy experience and the self-help group experience. It certainly is not always the borderline client that does the splitting. There is a segment of "purists" in AA, for example, that is antipsychotherapy and antipsychotropic medication. A borderline client caught between this variant of AA and ongoing therapy can be subject to a shame experience severe enough to threaten recovery. If such a circumstance develops, the clinician must be prepared to take either a protective or advocacy role relative to the client.

CLINICAL INDICATORS OF BPD

Psychoanalytically trained practitioners usually have relied primarily on the dynamics in the clinical relationship to diagnose a borderline condition. This heavy reliance on iatrogenic influences to make a diagnosis of BPD usually required several sessions.

With the publication of the DSM-III in 1980, clear diagnostic criteria for BPD became available for the first time. Clinicians now had a basis for reaching a diagnosis of BPD after a single clinical interview. These criteria were refined slightly in the DSM-III-R published in 1987. However, as Goldstein (1990, pp. 34–35) noted, the diagnostic criteria for BPD do not include any of the personality defense mechanisms considered by psychoanalysis as the defining features of the disorder. Central among these defenses is splitting.

The presence of splitting in a client's speech pattern can be an early indication in the initial clinical interview of a borderline condition. A trained and aware clinician almost always can diagnose BPD after one session with a client. The presence of splitting in a client's personality functioning is necessary for a diagnosis of BPD. The presence of splitting, however, is not sufficient to make a diagnosis of BPD because numerous other psychiatric conditions include splitting as a part of their dynamics.

Splitting, as noted in the section in this chapter on PTSD, is the psychoanalytic term for dissociation. Splitting, with its presumed origin in infancy, has been considered a "primitive defense" (Adler, 1985, p. 4). A more realistic understanding of splitting is that each stage of child and adult development includes forms of splitting. Splitting is not necessarily a "primitive" defense nor does it override or cancel out other psychological defenses as stated by psychoanalysis. However, splitting as a personality defense mechanism always distorts reality.

Splitting is a basic and pervasive psychological coping technique. People use splitting both for regulatory and defensive functions. Splitting is a basic technique both for initially organizing and separating psychological events. Because it is such a basic and pervasive psychological technique, splitting usually is not recognized by the person using the technique. It becomes a part of the way people view themselves, other people, and social relationships.

Any psychological content can be split in any way by individuals. Splitting, as a technique, actually includes a family of techniques. In its original psychoanalytic meaning, splitting was considered an exclusively unconscious process. In its revised meaning in this book, splitting may be conscious or unconscious.

The distinction between splitting as a psychological regulatory function and splitting as a psychological self-defense
function is crucial. A basic distinction between regulatory
splitting and self-defense splitting is that the former helps organize social reality while the latter distorts reality so as to
protect the individual psychologically. The distinction between the two types of splitting can be made clearer by knowing some of the outcomes.

One outcome from splitting as a regulatory function is that
it provides order to the self and to the environment. In one
sense splitting is at the core of Aristotelian logic in that this
form of logic splits the world into mutually exclusive categories. It is through this feature that regulatory splitting makes
a seminal contribution to ordering our selves and our reality.

A second outcome from regulatory splitting is the existence
of the necessary preconditions for sequencing psychological
events. The capability to do psychological sequencing is one
regulatory function that keeps individuals from becoming
overwhelmed psychologically. Splitting reality into separate
categories in which each category represents different events,
produces the capability of sequencing these categories along
some priority dimension. Once this priority dimension is in
place, individuals are better equipped to manage these
prioritized psychological events in a non-overwhelming way.

A third outcome from regulatory splitting is that the existing order and sequencing capabilities serve as prerequisites
for choicemaking by these individuals. Choicemaking is a key
psychological process for all human beings. This process requires both the skills to order and to sequence and an environment that can be ordered and sequenced. Choicemaking is
frequently an impaired process with people who have borderline personality disorder. Likewise, establishing and maintaining order and responding in a sequential and measured
manner often are compromised psychological skills for these
individuals.

A fourth outcome from regulatory splitting is the capability—assuming the presence of the three aforementioned outcomes—of individuals to exercise their psychological preferences. Such preferencing skills allow individuals to make
choices that reflect their psychological state (e.g. wants,

needs, desires, etc.) at the moment. Psychological preferencing is no longer a part of the regulatory splitting function when based on some other standard than the individual's psychological preference of the moment. Psychological preferencing can be differentiated from impulsive decision-making by the order associated with the former, and the disorder usually associated with the latter.

A fifth outcome from a pattern of regulatory splitting is the development of a template, or form, that provides some of the basic building blocks for a self. The four preceding outcomes all contribute to the psychological process of self development. Not surprisingly, the self is the core for psychological regulatory functions. One of the most basic self functions is to provide individuals with reliable distinctions within themselves (e.g. feelings, thoughts, beliefs, assumptions, facts, behaviors) and between themselves and others.

In fact, a sixth outcome of regulatory splitting is that individuals are able to maintain their selves while connecting interpersonally with the self of another individual. The absence of this type of interpersonal order (along with sequencing, choicemaking, and preferencing) leads to the now commonly recognized condition and process of codependency.

Self-defense splitting may represent both a skills deficit and a generic psychological style to protect one's self and social images. From psychological and interpersonal perspectives self-defense splitting always represents some degree of dysfunction or pathology. The severity of the splitting largely determines the severity of dysfunction of individuals.

The fundamental psychological deficit in self-defense splitting is twofold. First, psychological events are ordered (or split) not in a way that is representative of, or consistent with, social reality. Rather, the splitting or ordering occurs as a way individuals protect themselves from painful psychological realizations or awarenesses. Second, once individuals engage in this distorting or dysfunctional splitting, certain nonshared views or meanings about themselves, their relationships, and other people occur. Once these idiosyncratic views or meanings develop for individuals, it becomes very difficult to integrate or to reconcile these meanings with the views and meanings held by other people who do not rely on self-defensive splitting to order their psychological world.

Self-defense splitting leads to a good deal of chaos in people's lives because it seriously distorts how people prioritize psychological events. Prioritization is done to protect the individual's self-existence, self-identity or self-worth, not because of any order or priority based in reality. Thus, the use of self-defense splitting will create the impression that the person is self-centered, antagonistic, aloof, or not clearly in touch with "the way things are."

The problem with self-defense splitting is that the psychological safety it is supposed to provide is illusory in that individuals engaging in this type of splitting create new sources of psychological threat to themselves. The new sources of threat are mainly from other people who are split off from the meanings and views developed by an individual's self-defense splitting and who thus threaten the individual's reality orientation, social acceptance, or self-adequacy.

Self-defense splitting is a costly coping technique because its inherent psychologically isolating consequences generate significant abandonment, aggression/hostility, and shame issues. Because a view of self and others generated by self-defense splitting is not supported or reinforced interpersonally or socially, additional energy must be devoted to maintain the individual's distorted view.

Self-defense splitting is intended to keep individuals psychologically safe. An additional cost in using this coping technique, however, is that more advanced and more effective coping techniques are underused or underdeveloped. Two such compromised psychological coping techniques are reality-based choicemaking and preferencing. These more mature coping techniques serve developmental needs of individuals rather than provide defensive self protection. One set of needs choicemaking and preferencing serve is the timely development of self boundaries and functions.

Becoming aware of the use of self-defense splitting usually requires the help of a professional therapist. Table 2.1 shows a number of different types of splitting—both regulatory and self-defense.

"Splitting," as it is used here in the trauma-based concept

TABLE 2.1 Types of Splitting

Regulatory	Self-Defense
Biological	*Biological*
Induced vomiting is a way of getting rid of food that is spoiled and dangerous from the body.	Induced vomiting of bulimics is the splitting of normal food digestion from emotion-based eating.
Cognitive	*Cognitive*
The color red means to stop my car and can be frustrating, while the color green means to go in my car in an orderly way.	Red means someone is trying to frustrate me when I'm driving and green means I'm selected to get where I'm going with no hassle.
Emotional	*Emotional*
Although the parent's life was threatened, (s)he felt no fear or anxiety as (s)he rushed into the burning house to rescue the trapped 2-year-old child.	The adolescent was motionless and emotionally numb as the grandfather placed his hand on the adolescent's crotch.
Self	*Self*
In the midst of a verbal attack by an adolescent, the parent stepped back psychologically to say that these words were not a good measure of parental adequacy.	When the boss told the worker his work performance was not adequate, the worker merely shrugged his shoulders and said, "so?"
Behavioral	*Behavioral*
The therapist tells the parents he cannot discuss the feelings their child has expressed about them in therapy.	A client tells her therapist her spouse is wondering what is being said about him in her therapy.
Role	*Role*
The husband is a creative lover with his wife; he supervises his 7-year-old daughter's bath but does not wash her genitals.	As an employee, the person is quiet and compliant; as a parent, the person is verbally abusive and dominating.
Interpersonal	*Interpersonal*
The gynecologist reads Playboy magazine with his wife at home; he observes proper medical decorum in examining his patients.	In public the spouse is respectful and supportive to the other spouse; in private same spouse is physically abusive to his pre-teen child.

TABLE 2.1 Continued

Regulatory	Self-Defense
Spiritual	*Spiritual*
Sexual behavior judged by its "goodness" or "badness" based upon the commandment of adultery.	Sexual behavior judged by how good it feels and if it occurs between two consenting adults.

of BPD, has retained its core meaning of "dissociation" while changing its meaning in two other areas. Splitting is considered a family of coping techniques that manifest in at least eight areas: biological, cognitive, emotional, self, behavioral, role, interpersonal, and spiritual. The issue in splitting as a personality mechanism in BPD is not its "primitiveness" but which experiences are being distorted or dissociated. All adults employ splitting to some degree in coping with reality. It is not a coping technique limited to children and the severely psychologically impaired, as psychoanalysts sometimes state. Splitting may be either a healthy regulatory function or an unhealthy self-defense function.

The following is a checklist that clinicians can follow in assessing the presence and severity of defensive splitting in clients:

1. There is a clear separation of subjects that usually are integrated (e.g. "one parent was wonderful and the other was away from home a lot").
2. Oppositional style (e.g. client disagrees with most observations, explanations, or questions offered by the clinician).
3. Failure to accept mirroring (e.g. client avoids accepting the clinician's empathic responding, directly negates, or deflects clinician's compliments).
4. Triangulation (getting caught in the middle of two other people's needs, wants, disagreements) as a significant presenting problem or life pattern with the client.
5. Clients reveal a pattern of decision-making that is

based on pleasing other people rather than on the client's personal preference.

6. Clients reveal an "either-or" pattern in their thoughts, feelings, and behaviors.

7. Clients tend to talk about personal issues by using a "projective style" in which the pronouns "you," "she," and "he" predominate and "I" is used infrequently.

8. Client's speech pattern includes frequent use of passive voice when talking about a current life situation.

9. Clients reveal passive/idealizing/denigrating/ dependent themes when talking about themselves.

10. Clients are able to justify or accept their own behaviors and speech even when obviously harmful or counterproductive to their own best interests.

11. Clients reporting of a pattern of sexual, physical, or emotional abuse in childhood requires the clinician to assess carefully past and present existence of splitting.

These guidelines are intended to take a relatively parochial concept such as splitting and make it usable in a clinical setting for clinicians not trained or comfortable working from a psychoanalytic perspective.

REFERENCES

Adler, G. (1985). *Borderline psychopathology and its treatment.* Northvale, NJ: Jason Aronson.

American Psychiatric Association. (1987). *Diagnostic and statistical manual of mental disorders* (3rd edition-revised). Washington, DC: Author.

Bradshaw, J. (1988). *Healing the shame that binds you.* Deerfield Beach, FL: Health Communications, Inc.

Chatham, P. M. (1988). *Treatment of the borderline personality.* Northvale, NJ: Jason Aronson.

Counts, R. M. (1990). The concept of dissociation. *Journal of the American Academy of Psychoanalysis, 18* (3), 361.

Dulit, R. A., Fyer, M. R., Haas, G. G., Sullivan, T., & Frances, A. J. (1990). Substance use in borderline personality disorder. *American Journal of Psychiatry, 147* (8), 1003–1004.

Goldstein, E. G. (1990). *Borderline disorders*. New York: The Guilford Press.

Grotstein, J. (1981). *Splitting and projective identification*. New York: Aronson.

Gunderson, J. G., & Elliott, G. R. (1985). The interface between borderline personality disorder and affective disorder. *American Journal of Psychiatry, 142* (3), 278.

Hinsie, L. E., & Campbell, R. J. (1975). *Psychiatric Dictionary*. London: Oxford University Press.

Hoch, P., & Polatin, P. (1949). Pseudoneurotic forms of schizophrenia. *Psychiatric Quarterly, 23*, 249, 250.

Kaufman, G. (1989). *The psychology of shame*. New York: Springer Publishing Co.

Kernberg, O. (1967). Borderline personality organization. *Journal of the American Psychoanalytic Association, 15*, 641–685.

Kohut, H. (1977). *The restoration of the self*. New York: International Universities Press.

Kroll, J. (1988). *The challenge of the borderline patient*. New York: W. W. Norton & Co.

Langley, M. (1992). *A topology of splitting*. Unpublished paper.

Lewis, H. B. (1971). *Shame and guilt in neurosis*. New York: International Universities Press.

Mahler, M. S. (1971). A study of the separation-individuation process and its possible application to borderline phenomena in the psychoanalytic situation. *The Psychoanalytic Study of the Child, 26*, 403–424.

Masterson, J. F. (1981). *The narcissistic and borderline disorders*. New York: Brunner/Mazel.

Morrison, A. (1989). *Shame: The underside of narcissism*. Hillsdale, NJ: The Analytic Press.

Sansone, R. A., & Fine, M. A. (1992). Borderline personality as a predictor of outcome in women with eating disorders. *Journal of Personality Disorders, 6* (2), 183.

Schwartz, L. S. (1990). A biopsychosocial treatment approach to post-traumatic stress disorder. *Journal of Traumatic Stress, 3* (2), 221–238.

Skodol, A. E., & Oldham, J. M. (1991). Assessment and diagnosis of borderline personality disorder. *Hospital and Community Psychiatry, 42*, 10, 1021–1026.

Stone, A. M. (1992). The role of shame in post-traumatic stress disorder. *American Journal of Ortho-psychiatry, 62* (1), 131–136.

Tomkins, S. S. (1963). *Affect/imagery/consciousness: Vol. 2, the negative affects*. New York: Springer Publishing Co.

Tomkins, S. S. (1982). Affect theory. In P. Elsman (Ed.), *Emotions in the human face* (2nd ed: pp. 353–395). Cambridge, England: Cambridge University Press.

Tomkins, S. S. (1987). Script theory. In J. Aronoff, A. I. Rubin, & R. A. Zucker (Eds.), *The emergence of personality*. New York: Springer Publishing Co.

van der Kolk, B. A., Brown, P., & van der Hart, O. (1989). Pierre Janet on post-traumatic stress. *Journal of Traumatic Stress, 2* (4), 365–378.

Westen, D. (1990). Towards a revised theory of borderline object relations: Contributions of empirical research. *International Journal of Psycho-Analysis, 71,* 661–693.

Wolf, E. S. (1988). *Treating the self: Elements of clinical self psychology*. New York: The Guilford Press.

Shame: The Core Emotion in Borderline Personality Disorder

3

I n the preceding chapter splitting was shown to have both a regulatory and a defensive function. A similar distinction holds true for shame. Bradshaw distinguishes between healthy and toxic shame. Healthy shame signals our limits as human beings and serves as a reality-based limit on our grandiosity or sense of omnipotence. Toxic shame is experienced as a generalized sense of being flawed and defective (Bradshaw, 1988, pp. 4, 10). The shame that produces BPD is toxic.

The concept of shame that is a part of the self-management theory of BPD is closer to Tomkins biopsychosocial concept than it is to a psychoanalytic concept. The psychoanalytic concept sees shame occurring as a result of a deficit between individuals' views of themselves and their ego ideals (or their superegos, for some authors) (Morrison, 1989, pp. 3, 11). Tomkins' concept of shame is that shame is one of nine affects with which individuals are born. At birth shame is a "primary innate biological motivating mechanism" that develops psychological and social dimensions as the individual grows (Tomkins, 1987, p. 137).

With Tomkins' concept of shame there is a basis for biological, psychological, and social dimensions. There are two aspects of shame that are highly relevant to BPD. One, shame is an auxiliary affect; that is, shame occurs by inhibiting either the full occurrence or expression of interest or excitement. In describing Tomkins' concept of shame, Kaufman (1989, p. 30) notes, "shame is an affect auxiliary because it operates only after the positive affects, interest or enjoyment, have been activated." In this manner shame can occur from sources within the individual or from environmental sources.

In addition to shame having innate activations within individuals, it also can be activated interpersonally. Kaufman (1989, p. 12) uses the term "interpersonal bridge" to refer to the emotional bond that ties any two people together no matter for how long, at what level of intensity, or for what reason. As Kaufman notes, an interpersonal bridge forms out of reciprocal interest and shared experiences of trust. It is for this reason that mistaking a total stranger for a close friend, speaking only to be ignored, can be such a shaming experience. The shunting by the stranger is the incomplete inhibition of interest or excitement that produces the shame (sometimes experienced as feeling "silly" or "dumb") experience.

A second aspect of shame that is highly relevant to BPD is the binding capability of the shame experience. According to Tomkins, affects provide the meaning and the intensity of experiences. Through the laws of learning any affect can bind or become associated with any experience or any other affect. This binding capability of shame has particular significance for understanding BPD. Shame is a derivative or cost associated with the development of identity. In fact, the development of the self occurs, in part, through the dialectical relationship between shame and narcissism. As will be noted in subsequent sections of this chapter, the binding capability of shame greatly affects both its recognition and its expression by the individual.

Because of the many manifestations of shame, a clinically useful definition is elusive. Wurmser combined affect theory and psychoanalytic theory and reached the following cognitively based definition of shame:

> Shame is a fairly defined affect . . . caused by a discrepancy between expectancy and realization: an inner or an outer conflict. It is the polarity, the tension, between how I want to be seen and how I am . . . The higher the self-expectation and the greater the demand for perfection, the harsher the need for

self-chastisement by self-ridicule, self-scorn and by symbolic or real disappearance and self-effacement. Insofar as 'narcissism' refers to the concept of 'self-esteem,' and 'pathological narcissism' [refers] to . . . 'overevaluation' of oneself or of others (something 'immoderate,' 'limitless') . . . any great discrepancy between self-expectation ('ideal self') and self-perception ('real self') is by definition a narcissistic conflict . . . that is felt as shame. (1987, p. 76)

Shame does not have a significant role in the psychoanalytic concept of BPD. The psychoanalytic treatment of BPD aims to dissolve the blocked aggression that has inhibited the development of object constancy (the integration of positive and negative elements of an experience or person) in individuals with BPD.

The self-management therapy model of BPD described in this book has as a major objective the improvement of self-efficacy in borderline clients. Briefly, self-efficacy consists of two central dimensions—outcome expectations and efficacy expectations. Outcome expectations are the person's belief that particular behaviors will achieve a certain outcome. Efficacy expectations are individuals' beliefs that they can execute successfully the behaviors that will achieve the desired outcome. Any significant negative discrepancy between the desired and actual outcome will cause shame. The negative discrepancy will cause the individual to have a partial reduction in interest or excitement about the outcome *per se* or individuals' belief in their capability of achieving the outcomes. Shame is the direct consequence of the incomplete reduction of expectations associated with inadequate behaviors or with expectations that are unrealistically high. Shame occurs because of individuals believing they are inadequate, incompetent, insignificant, irrelevant, impotent, or inept due to their own fault. The rest of this chapter will provide a detailed discussion of shame.

HOW DOES SHAME DEVELOP?

A common feature of a shame experience is for individuals to look immediately to see if anybody noticed or to feel some relief if they know they were alone when the shameful experience occurred. Why the exposure issue or the presence of an observer is so important probably goes to the heart of how toxic shame develops.

This book considers shame to be an inherent part of social psychological experiences. Healthy shame functions as a protective barrier in which we recognize our limitations as individuals. In so recognizing our limitations we avoid situations that are dangerous or not satisfying to us. For example, it is healthy shame that is associated with not walking onto a busy street without checking for traffic, rejecting a dangerous dare by a friend, or interrupting a marathon run because of not feeling well. Healthy shame is associated with self-regulatory decisions we make about ourselves, our behaviors or our lifestyles.

Toxic shame, on the other hand, is a self-defense condition that occurs when individuals experience inadequacy, insignificance, ineptness, irrelevancy or impotence. Toxic shame is associated with a sense of deficiency. This section will describe how toxic shame (hereafter referred to as "shame") develops in infancy and takes various age appropriate forms throughout the lifespan.

Shame can be understood as developing out of the symbiotic phase of infancy which occurs during the first 5 or 6 months of life. During this phase the infant becomes fused psychologically with the caregiver, but not completely fused. Physical as well as psychological sustenance flows from the caregiver to the infant and subsequently from the infant back to the caregiver. Mahler (1971, p. 411) describes this condition as "narcissistically fused."

The precursors of shame may begin during this phase as nonverbal body sensations associated with the "inadequate" symbiotic fusion. It is likely that these "proto-shame" experiences occur as a result of the naturally occurring, less than optimally satisfying interactions between caregiver and infant; interactions that reinforce the symbiotic relationship are experienced as "good" by the infant and interactions that are not conducive to full symbiosis are experienced as "bad." Because of developmental limitations of the infant, it is likely that such bad feeling experiences are the basis of healthy shame as the infant encounters the inadequacies of symbiosis and the unavoidable necessity of separateness. It simply is not possible to fuse completely or perfectly with the caregiver, nor is it even in the infant's best interest to do so.

If healthy shame results from the incipient separation that necessarily occurs with inadequate symbiosis, it is less clear when toxic shame becomes developmentally possible. If dissatisfaction is the basis of healthy shame, then fault, personal deficiency, frustration, or dissatisfaction seem to be the basis of toxic shame. It is not clear at what age young children transform healthy shame into toxic shame. It most certainly is some time after the child has developed at least the rudimentary boundary setting skills associated with the separation–individuation phase described so well by Mahler (1971) because of the cognitive and social demands inherent in toxic shame.

Shame is associated closely with the development of the self. The self is shaped by the interaction within the individual of narcissism and shame. The interpenetration of these positive (narcissism) and negative (shame) forces from repeated interactions with individuals and events leads to the psychological structure and function we call the self. Presumably the self is uniquely human. The presence of a self allows humans to treat themselves as social objects. Mediated by language, a person's "I" (subjective) can react to themselves—to their "me." It is this regulatory split in the self that makes self-consciousness possible. It is toward the "me," which is the accumulated self-identity of the individual, that individuals develop expectations for themselves. It is the interest and excitement that develop toward "me" activities, goals, and beliefs that can generate shame when this interest and excitement are associated with failed or inadequate behavior. For purposes of understanding the role of shame in BPD, the following description illustrates how shame may occur:

1. Individuals experience a partial reduction in some personally relevant interest or excitement because of other individuals' behavior.
2. The partial reduction condition creates a temporary state of ambivalence experienced as cognitive confusion, emotional numbness, or self-doubt.

3. The unmet expectations associated with the partial re-
    duction condition create a psychological deficiency
    condition of either too high expectations or too inade-
    quate behavior. At this point the shame experience has
    occurred for the individual and the self has lost some
    of its clarity and worth.
4. To seek relief from the deficiency condition, individuals
    project themselves into the role of the "other" to see if
    this reference person or group could be expected to
    have this same partial reduction in interest or excite-
    ment experience or if the person or group shows less in-
    terest in the individual. It is in this step that the shame
    experience dilutes or hardens the interpersonal bound-
    aries that result in merging or isolating.
5. Toxic shame seems to be the result of the shamed indi-
    vidual accepting fault for the partial reduction in inter-
    est and excitement.

Of course, the shame experience in reality is virtually never
as rational and orderly as this description suggests. A shame
experience may be either conscious or unconscious, it may be
verbal or non-verbal and it may be accurately or inaccurately
labeled. The distinguishing feature of a shame experience is
reduced clarity about the self (self-identity) or reduced worth
about the self (self-esteem).

It is Step 4 in the shame process where splitting occurs. As
noted previously, splitting entails a family of responses. Thus, in
addition to splitting being an interpersonal process, splitting
also can be an intra-personal process. Shame can occur relative
to an external audience or it can occur relative to an individual's
expectation or ideal. In this shame scenario in Step 4, the vulnerable or exposed individual transfers very temporarily to the audience person the initiative to define the shamed person as adequate or as meaningful. Shame occurs for the first person if s/he
believes the other's perception is a devaluation.

Two features of this shame process are especially significant. Shame requires an audience—real or psychological.
Second, shame involves a collapse or a dilution of self/other
boundaries as self or social identity is brought into question.
It is the pressure on the person's self-boundaries that causes

shame to split the self or other psychological experiences. It is the centrality of shame to self and identity that helps account for its painful searing feature. As Kaufman (1989, p. 8) notes, shame is associated with an inferior feeling or belief state. In the following quote, Kaufman establishes the breadth of consequences to the self caused by shame:

> Because shame is central to conscience, indignity, identity and disturbances in self-functioning, this affect is the source of low self-esteem, poor self-concept or body image, self-doubt and insecurity and diminished self-confidence. Shame is the affect that is the source of feelings of inferiority. The inner experience of shame is like a sickness within the self. (1989, pp. 5–6)

The use of shame in self-management therapy for BPD differs in several ways from its psychoanalytic use. Psychoanalytically, shame is considered to be a primitive and infantile emotion, a precursor to the more complicated emotion of guilt. Morrison, in his review of the major psychoanalytic writings on shame, summarizes Frances Broucek's concept:

> Broucek suggested that shame is the fundamental painful affect encountered in narcissistic personalities [such as BPD]. . . . [He] connected shame with disappointment in the hoped-for response of the parental [caretaking] environment to the infant's communicated pleasurable behavior. [Shame] represents, as well, environmental feedback suggesting incompetence, inefficacy and the inability to influence, predict or comprehend an event which the infant expected . . . to be able to control or to understand. . . . Broucek considered shame to play a double role in narcissism and the grandiose self: as an instigator in the (defensive) creation of the grandiose self and as a ego response to grandiosity, leading to the splitting off of the grandiose self from the core self organization. (1989, pp. 53–54)

As used in self-management therapy shame is not considered either primitive or infantile. It is an emotion with a complex mixture of cognitive, emotional, physical, and interpersonal components. It is an emotion that occurs across the lifespan. Perhaps the key feature of shame is its self-identity and self-disruption quality. It is this disruption feature that makes it a core part and a core consequence of any traumatic experience. The "jolt" or shock quality that is so often a feature of shame experiences may be the tearing impact of a shame experience colliding with the dynamic tension present in the self. This tearing experience may be the disruption of self-continuity as it is unable to integrate the shame experience. This failure to integrate the shame experience into the self leaves the shame experience split off and having to be managed by another psychological system. It is probably in this manner that a false "self" develops. This false self can be experience-specific or it can take on a systemic quality and manage a wide range of experience that, over time, compete with the "real" self as to the individual's "real" identity.

As noted earlier, shame as used in the self-management model of BPD has both psychological and social dimensions to it. Splitting is a psychological form of toxic shame. Projective identification, a frequently used defense mechanism in BPD, represents a social form of toxic shame. This concept of projective identification has a plethora of meanings in the clinical literature, but can be reduced to three core steps:

1. Person A projects an unwanted psychological condition or state onto Person B.
2. Person B acts in a manner consistent with the condition or state projected by Person A.
3. Person A introjects in a form revised by Person B the condition or state originally projected by Person A but made more palatable by Person B.

All projective identifications (PI) in individuals with BPD are shame driven. PI may be conscious or unconscious, aware or unaware, intentional or non-intentional. While splitting can occur with one individual or between several, PI requires at least two people in order to occur.

HOW IS SHAME RECOGNIZED?

Both phenomenologically and clinically shame can be very difficult to recognize. Lewis acknowledges the presence of unlabeled shame in an individual:

... states of shame and guilt often exist without being correctly identified by the patient. In addition, shame is often unacknowledged because it is extremely painful and perceived as irrational. There is also a state I call 'bypassed' shame in which events that might evoke shame are registered or noted by a 'wince' or 'jolt' to the self . . . The ideation following bypassed shame is often difficult to distinguish from guilty ideation. Acute, unidentified, or unacknowledged shame is often hard to distinguish from its rapid transformation into depressive ideation. (1987, p. 107)

The presence of shame unlabeled, the splitting consequences of shame that allow the emotion to bypass awareness, and the changing unstable nature of shame all make it difficult to recognize a shame experience. The numerous forms that shame takes add to the difficulty of accurate phenomenological or clinical recognition. Lewis notes that there are numerous varieties of shame that need to be identified:

Mortification, humiliation, embarrassment, feeling ridiculous, chagrin, shyness and modesty are all different psychological states, but with the common property of being directly about the self. . . . I treat them as variants of the shame family, but with different admixtures of pride and self-directed hostility. (1987, p. 110)

Denial seems to play a major role in blocking individual awareness of shame experience. Lewis describes:

Difficulties in identifying one's own experience as shame have so often been observed that they suggest some intrinsic connection between shame and the mechanism of denial. Denial seems to function in at least two ways, depending on the availability or overtness of affect. In the first pattern of denial shame affect is overt or available to consciousness but the person experiencing it either will not or cannot identify it. (1987, p. 196)

The second kind of shame denial is the aforementioned bypassed shame, in which the cognitive component is blanked out of the person's awareness but shame is experienced as a "wince" or "jolt."

Lewis (1987, p. 276) has identified 11 sequences of shame

that connect "overt, unidentified shame feeling with depression, via undischarged guilt for shame-rage." Wurmser talks about the role of screen affects as effective defenses against shame. It should be noted that defense against shame usually involves unawareness or a distracting emotional facade that blocks a person's sense of shame. Wurmser describes these emotional facades or defenses:

> Most frequently this is performed by anger and rage. Then we have scorn: to show up others as contemptible and ridiculous instead of oneself. There is haughtiness: in cold arrogance or icy withdrawal one fights off the hurt of shame and engages in all those grandiose claims and fantasies now so often lumped together as narcissism. There may be hubris, the wanton disregard for the sensitivity of others. Spite, or defiance, is one of the most important affect defenses . . . and one can engage in lying and other forms of trying to defeat authority within and without in order not to feel shame. Where there is envy you will find shame underneath. Numbness, the stony mask of alexithymia, may often be a defense against the most profound shame by the freezing of all feelings. (1987, pp. 86–87)

Lewis (1971, p. 110) adds the important affect defense of humor as another way of distracting attention or awareness from shame.

Introspection is of very limited value in identifying shame. Because of the centrality of splitting in the shame experience, the help of a professional therapist who is aware of shame dynamics and shame defenses is usually necessary to help clients recognize their shame.

In Wurmser's list of affect defenses against shame it is easy to recognize defenses employed by many borderline clients in clinical settings. It is hoped that recognition by clinicians that their borderline clients are protecting themselves from shame awareness will mitigate the disruptive iatrogenic forces that so often threaten the therapy of borderline clients. Clearly, if clinicians are not aware of the influence of shame on their clients and on the client/clinician relationship, the outbursts that eventually occur with borderline clients won't be seen by clinicians as the self-protective behaviors they are. These same clinicians also will be unaware of the iatrogenic shame dynamics operating in the therapy relationship.

With borderline clients it is important to remember that such clients frequently have undiagnosed PTSD. Thus, with a trauma-based model of BPD, the search for shame cannot be restricted to the caretaking experiences clients received from their parents. While there is very often unresolved abandonment trauma with either the father or the mother, there often are specific shame-inducing traumatic experiences outside the family of origin that have to be identified, labeled as to their shame, and then integrated into the person's perception of him or herself.

The presence of clinical levels of depression often coexists with toxic levels of shame. The clinical folk wisdom that depression is anger turned inward is only partially true. Depression also can result from shame. Lewis describes the relationship between depression and shame in the following manner:

> Evidence from cognitive and behavioral approaches to depression strongly suggests the usefulness of considering shame as a major component of depression. In a reformulation of learned helplessness theory, Abramson, Seligman and Teasdale suggest that depression is the end product of a faulty attributional style in which people focus on their personal helplessness. Specifically, learned helplessness theory assumes that people who attribute the causes of 'bad events' to 'internal', 'stable', and 'global' personal traits . . . are likely to be depressed.
> . . . Peterson, Schwartz and Seligman found that depressed women undergraduates were more likely to blame their *characters* for bad events than they were to blame specific *behaviors*. . . . If we equate blame of the self for its character with shame and blame for behaviors with guilt, we [have] a convergence of evidence from behavioral and psychoanalytic sources suggesting the role of shame in depression. (1987, pp. 105–106)

Many of the defenses that make it difficult to recognize shame also make it difficult to express shame. Considerable time is spent in self-management therapy helping borderline clients recognize and label their shame. A fairly typical process clients follow in shame recognition work is to go from unawareness, to passive denial, to passive acceptance, to active denial and rebuttal, to overt resistance and anger. It is this phase of self-management therapy that places the most stress on the therapist and client. The therapist is confronting the core problem in the client's BPD—bringing to the client's awareness the level of toxic shame. In return, the client frequently uses denial and projective identification as ways to avoid such self-knowledge. Confrontation, as opposed to low-key repetitiveness during this phase of therapy, is usually counter-productive. By its very nature toxic shame is pervasive in a borderline person's psychological makeup. Thus, it is not critical to break through a client's denial of their shame on any one subject. Denial of shame is dissolved over time by helping clients see the pervasiveness and varieties of their shame experiences.

HOW IS SHAME EXPRESSED?

Tomkins' biopsychosocial concept of shame, used in this book, means that shame can manifest itself in numerous ways. For clinical purposes shame can be expressed at one of six levels—biological or physical, emotional, cognitive, behavioral, interpersonal, and social. Two caveats should be kept in mind for clinicians who are exploring the shame dynamics of clients. All shame-related experiences impact the self and no shame experience shows itself at only one of the six levels. Rather, the clinical significance of identifying a particular level of toxic shame expression is to help the clinician link a specific pattern of toxic shame to an identifiable self disorder and to link the presence of toxic shame with specific experiences encountered by the client.

The second caveat is that nobody has a "pure" shame experience. For a host of reasons—shame as an auxiliary affect, its binding capability to other emotions, its close connection to denial, its unlabeled state, its fluid nature—shame usually is an experience mixed with other emotions. It is for these reasons that the psychoeducation of clients about their toxic shame is so important therapeutically. As an emotion shame has obvious mind-body connections. Shame can be expressed in a myriad of ways in a clinical setting. It behooves the clinician to be aware of the range of shame manifestations.

Shame as a biological or physical expression can occur in any one of several physical systems in the body. For example, the altered appetite and eating difficulties of individuals with clinical level eating disorders may be based in unrecognized or unresolved shame. At less dramatic levels, shame, in the form of embarrassment or lack of confidence, may lead to stuttering speech or a stumble or a trip while walking in front of an audience. Shame about shame can release a plethora of autonomic nervous system functions such as sweaty palms, dry mouth and blushing. The occurrence of these characteristics easily can lead to shame being mislabeled as anxiety.

The high percentage of borderline clients who are addicted to food, alcohol, and drugs speaks clearly to a biological or physical manifestation of shame. Other physical manifestations that suggest the presence of shame include lowering of the eyes or head, a significant slump of the shoulders, or a significant reduction in the loudness of a person's speech.

Shame is much more diverse in its expression than is, for example, anger. Shame refers to a family of emotions in which the nuances of feeling are sufficiently different to cover their commonality. Embarrassment, humiliation, mortification, and shyness are only four variants of shame. Due to mislabeling and nonlabeling, clients often misunderstand or are unaware of their shame experiences. The most common type of mislabeling seems to be confusing "guilt" with "shame." However, because of the binding capability of shame to other emotions, virtually any emotion can serve as a front or defense against shame awareness.

Very little has been written about the long half life of the shame emotion. While anger is a spike emotion that can complete its full cycle of expression in seconds, if the situation warrants, shame is very different. The half-life of shame can be decades. For example, many people avoid their high school reunions presumably because of shame issues. The manner in which shame occurs—the partial reduction of interest and excitement—creates a memory trace that easily can be stored in the conscious or unconscious. Invoking the Zeigarnik effect—noncompleted experiences are recalled more quickly than completed experiences—there is a psychological basis for the enduring nature of shame. Shame retains its potency, in part, because of its unspent or unexpressed energy. Shame also retains its potency over time because of its close association with the self. Shame—recent or past—can influence all aspects of the self and its functioning.

Therapeutically, much psychoeducational work must be done with borderline clients to help them identify their shame experiences. These clients frequently comment on the relative intensity of a shame memory, sometimes years after the original experience. Unlike anger, again more of a spike emotion, shame tapers off in its intensity at a much slower rate. In understanding how shame occurs, it is important to remember that shame is the result of the incomplete reduction of interest or excitement in a specific subject, or the breaking of an interpersonal bridge that consists largely of shared expectations between people. Consequently the remnants of partially reduced interest or excitement, or the rupture of an existing interpersonal relationship, extend the length of an emotional shame experience.

The cognitive manifestations of shame share in common a disruption in continuity of thought, speech, or perception. The most innocuous cognitive indicator of shame may be a person's confusion in the meaning of an incident, encounter, or word. Of course, not all instances of confusion indicate a shame experience. A break in one's train of thought, or a malapropism, also can be possible indicators of unaware or unlabeled shame.

Shame seems closely associated with the psychological process of splitting. The emotional splitting in shame appears to occur through psychic numbing. The cognitive splitting in shame seems to occur by a disruption in the train of thought or by "drawing a blank." Again, shame seems imminently compatible with splitting because of the way shame occurs. Because of the partial reduction of interest and excitement, as the basis for the shame, occurrence of a person experiencing shame can focus on one of two conditions. The focus, which can happen with or without awareness, can be on the remaining interest and excitement, producing an experience of curiosity or challenge. Or, the focus can be on the lost interest and excitement, producing an experience of shame. The wide gradations of shame that are possible are probably related to the level of partial reduction that occurs in the interest and excitement directed toward a subject.

The partial reduction in interest and excitement toward an object is a necessary but usually not a sufficient condition to trigger a shame experience. There are several additional factors—observer characteristics, significance of subject, current psychological state of the person, etc.—that will influence whether shame occurs and how intense the occurrence will be.

The evolution of the term "borderline" from the 1930s to the 1990s has seen an emphasis on the emotional or affective characteristics of BPD and a de-emphasis on the cognitive characteristics of BPD. At one point the cognitive characteristics of BPD were referred to as "brief psychotic episodes." These episodes could include instances of depersonalization (people temporarily believing they are not themselves in a stressful situation), derealization (temporarily believing that real world conditions really are not happening), or significant minimization or denial. Cognitive characteristics are no longer used in reaching a BPD diagnosis.

With the publication of DSM-IV in early 1994, it is likely that diagnostic recognition will be given to dissociation features of a less severe nature than psychotic. In this way the cognitive/perceptual distortions are receiving renewed interest in diagnosing BPD.

The cognitive/perceptual dimension of shame usually is easy to connect to splitting, but is much more difficult to connect to shame. It is important for clinicians to remember the disguised fronts that borderline clients use to hide their shame, the importance initially to respect the shame defenses, and the significant possibilities of iatrogenically induced shame from the therapy experience. A seemingly insignificant misunderstanding or misperception between clinician and client can trigger a moderate to major shame attack. Clearly a clinician sensitized to expect a blow up from borderline clients is likely to miss the client's precipitating shame experience.

Behaviors associated with incompetency or ineffectiveness, with the incomplete suppression of interest or excitement, or with the breaking of an interpersonal trust bridge can be expected to produce shame. For each of these three classes of behaviors, the type and intensity of shame is likely to differ. Failure to get a raise at work, failure to make the school's athletic team, failure to understand your spouse's feelings, failure to win an election in your church or civic group, or simply being accused or presumed to be inadequate, whether you are or are not, are all instances of shame-inducing behavior. It is significant that the behavior that induces shame in a person may be either your own behavior or somebody's behavior toward you. Shame-inducing behavior requires a real or perceived audience. In fact, one such audience can be the self as it assesses the impact of the behavior on it own image.

Upon reflection it is easy to see how the behaviors discussed above induce shame. The shame generation component in behavior that partially suppresses interest or excitement is sometimes more difficult to understand. Telling a joke to another person who does not find it funny, being told to calm down, being told to stop feeling, thinking, or behaving a certain way, mistaking a stranger for a friend, calling a friend by another friend's name, are all instances of partially suppressed interest or excitement. What is confusing to some people is how genuine behavior that includes honest mistakes still can produce shame. Such behavior is shame-inducing because of the incomplete suppression of interest or excitement.

Shame produced by partially suppressed excitement or interest is particularly likely to happen in psychotherapy with borderline clients. Through the perceptual/cognitive distortion of therapist idealization, borderline clients often seem to expect near perfect mirroring by the therapist. While failure to get such mirroring can be frustrating and anger-producing for the client, it is first and foremost shameful because clients typically get less than perfect mirroring from their therapists. Such imperfect mirroring can leave these clients feeling irrelevant or insignificant.

The third class of shame-inducing behaviors—breaking of an interpersonal trust bridge—actually spills over into the interpersonal level of shame. These behaviors require a preexisting relationship that is violated by either party. Talking about your spouse in a private way with another person and the spouse learns about it, learning that your best friend has made sexual advances toward your significant other, realizing someone is using you while pretending that a special relationship exists, believing a valued employee is stealing from you, are all instances of shaming behaviors caused by the breaking of the trust bridge. It is important to realize that the trust between two people need not be reciprocal in order for shame to occur. The trust condition is subjective and one or the other person only must *think* that the trust condition exists in order for shame to occur.

Individuals with BPD are particularly prone to interpret disapproval of their behavior as shameful statements or personal rejections. It is just such a misperception that can generate a rage reaction in the borderline person and can threaten self-esteem along with threatening an important social or clinical relationship. It is clear to this clinician that splitting and shame are impacting the self of borderline individuals in such circumstances. Exactly what the process involves in this shaming/rejecting impact is not clear. Because such outbursts seem so common in clinical settings by individuals with BPD, some speculation of what is happening may be helpful.

A normally functioning self is organized by a regulatory split into a subjective self (the "I") and an objective self (the "me"). The "I" is the willful initiating part of the self while the "me" is the residue of experiences that makes up the identity part of the self. Individuals with BPD also have this regulatory split in their selves. The me, or the identity part of the self, is an instance of object constancy and is another example of why the object relations theory of BPD is in error. Because of the presence of self-identity, individuals are able to respond to themselves as they respond to other individuals. It is this reflexive quality of the self that differentiates humans from animals. An individual with BPD who physically harms herself intentionally is an example of the "I" and "me" working together.

What seems to make individuals with BPD different is the role that defensive splitting and shame play in the functioning of the self. Individuals with a BPD have very poor self-esteem and very diffuse self-identity. So borderline individuals clearly distinguish themselves (object self) from other people (something individuals with a psychotic disorder cannot do reliably). However, borderline individuals, with their diffuse identity, are unable to manage negative speech or behavior directed toward them. It seems that the combination of low self-esteem and diffuse identity requires the shaming speech or behavior (the negative quality serves to reduce partially the individuals interest or excitement about themselves) to be split off defensively or self-protectively. The defensive splitting seems to be necessary because the diffuse identity of the borderline individual is unable to contain or to direct the speech or behavior to the relevant part of the individual's self. Instead, borderline individuals seem to encounter the negative speech/behavior as directed against the whole self. The withdrawn, angry, or rageful response that follows by the borderline individual seems defensive in two ways. First, the defensiveness is a response that hides the shame that is the more core and debilitating emotion in the experience. Second, the defensiveness seems to be a reaction against the injustice of being uniformly devalued as an individual. The injustice is reality-oriented but the borderline individual's misperception of being globally devalued often is not an accurate perception of reality. If this description is accurate, the clinician must anticipate when borderline clients have these experiences in therapy and proactively defuse them through reframing and psychoeducating.

The last level of shame is social or cultural. This pertains to the meanings or symbols, norms and values, and institutional practices associated with how our society establishes the value of individuals and maintains order between individuals and groups. Until very recently there was at least the belief that sexual activity was regulated by the institution of marriage, that obedience to criminal law was regulated by the criminal justice system, and that wealth was acquired through licensed and legitimate business. Any violation of these norms, values, or institutional procedures brought great shame on the transgressor. In addition it used to be that using illegal drugs or getting caught using them was very shameful.

There are many mediating variables between the functioning of institutions and the functioning of individuals. If, in fact, BPD is one of the rising psychiatric disorders of the 1990s, the co-occurrence of splitting in most of our major social institutions may not be simply coincidental. The splitting of marriages and families long has been evidenced by divorce statistics. With the demise of the neighborhood school, childrens' lives often are split between two very different sections of their town. With so many two-income families, many childrens' lives after school also are split into two locations, with two very different sets of rules. This kind of split living often produces discontinuities that become difficult to integrate into existing self systems.

Significant discontinuities. or splits, also have developed in adult lives. Work careers are no longer continuous. Some adults already have two to three careers during their work lives. The shame potential associated with "starting over" can be quite significant.

Work organizations no longer provide employees with continuity. With the advent of the global economy, companies must manage their human resources as tightly as they do any other function in the organization. Longevity, formerly a hard-earned resource, has become a major liability. Very often the longer you have worked for an organization, the more expensive and expendable you become. The shame associated with being treated as superfluous is usually considerable. If the pervasiveness of splitting of traditional institutions continues, the capacity for individuals to experience shame could be affected permanently. If our interest and excitement in having membership in various normative organizations are replaced by a type of functional necessity, there will be a corresponding drop in the presence or intensity of shame. If there is a connection between shame and social control, a loss in the capability of institutions to induce shame will produce a loss in social control.

When one looks at the U.S. society of the 1990s, much of the culture's capacity to induce shame has been diluted. It is an exaggeration to say we are becoming a shameless society. Rather, what seems to be happening is that shame is becoming highly individualized. It may be that one form this individualizing of shame is taking is that it is becoming highly "psychopathologized." Subsequent research and social analysis are needed before this point can be accepted as accurate.

SHAME AND DENIAL

The psychoanalyst Helen Block Lewis was quoted earlier in this chapter as suggesting some intrinsic connection between shame and denial. According to Lewis, one form of shame-induced denial is an inability to identify the shame experience verbally. A second kind of shame experience is a wordless "jolt" or "wince." A third kind of denial of shame experience is a denial of reality or consequences. This third type of shame denial often is associated with addictive behavior.

In its most subtle form shame denial can occur as an experience of mislabeling. Shame might be described as guilt. In its more moderate form shame denial may take the form of a particular and incomplete cause and effect description. For example, a person who had too much to drink and whose car hit a guard rail may see the accident as caused solely by a wet highway, poor signage, worn tires, etc. Their alcohol-induced incompetence is denied as a causative factor. The most florid form of shame denial is straightforward rejection of reality or lying about reality. An example of this type of shame denial would be the borderline client who purposefully cuts herself and then denies the cut is harmful or intentional.

The shame denial of borderline patients requires a great deal of persistence and restraint on the part of the clinician. Unmasking the shame involves a series of probes. To make an initial appraisal of shame, clinicians simply can ask clients if they are aware of being shamed in a particular instance. Listening to the response will tell the clinician if shame is present in subtle, moderate or florid form and if shame is present, the types of shame masks the client might be using. The clinician should make note of these masks because this information will be useful in later interventions. It has been my experience that many clients have trouble using the word "shame" or having it used to describe their experience. Such resistance is a subtle type of shame denial. Though subtle, such shame denial does not dissolve easily or quickly through clinical intervention. The intervention most frequently used in self-management therapy is psychoeducation in which the various dimensions of the shame experience (emotional, cognitive, behavioral, interpersonal, etc.) are labeled verbally for the client.

If the clinician and client successfully dissolve the shame denial, the next step is to explore why or how the client developed this denial. The goal in this step is twofold. First, clients are encouraged to look at some of the significant shaming relationships in their present and past. Second, they are shown the relationships between shame, shame denial, self-image, self-protection, and their BPD. Shame denial can derail this discussion, as some borderline clients will not acknowledge the presence of shame and the sense of psychological vulnerability that it produces.

Included in this chapter is a list of shame defenses developed by Leon Wurmser. Familiarity with this list can assist the clinician greatly in helping clients dissolve shame denial. It is important to remember that dissolving shame denial is only the beginning phase of shame integration work with borderline clients.

If client resistance to shame denial cannot be dissolved, a less direct approach to toxic shame is possible. The role of healthy shame can be discussed and identified. Healthy shame essentially establishes our limits as a species and as individuals. The aversion or "jolt" potential that is so much a part of the shame experience and shame awareness can be somewhat reduced for clients by showing the vital role healthy shame plays in establishing personal limitations. For example, it is healthy shame that helps us accept that we decline to fight a much larger and stronger person, that we cannot be everybody's best friend, or that our own death is inevitable. The concept that provides a transition from healthy shame to toxic shame is that of "fault," "deficiency," "inadequacy," etc. These deficit conditions are lacking in healthy shame.

Shame work with borderline clients may be an unending task. The goal in self-management therapy is simply to get a good enough understanding of toxic shame in order for it to be self managed by clients at an adequate level.

The possibility of an iatrogenic-produced shame experience by the clinician is very real when working with borderline clients. The clinician conducting shame reduction work with a borderline client is not unlike a munitions expert trying to defuse a live bomb. Secrets, silence, and isolation are three conditions that generate and sustain shame. Each of these conditions is a type of shame denial. It is perhaps the pervasiveness of these conditions in the perpetration of shame that makes talking about shameful subjects so healing.

It is important to note that secrecy, silence, and isolation often are defenses against secondary shame. The silence that incest victims exercise in hiding their traumatic experiences from other people provides these victims with some shame protection with respect to contemporary relationships. This shame protection is concerned with secondary shame. However, the primary shame associated with the original incest experience still must be addressed, even after the silence and isolation around secondary shame are removed. It is likely that a major difference between primary and secondary toxic shame is the presence of PTSD in the former.

There are instances clinically when the borderline client's shame defenses are impenetrable. Such clients often combine rigid emotional splitting with a great deal of intellectualization. In such instances the clinician might try discussing the concept of inferiority as the client applies it to him or herself. Such a discussion could proceed toward asking clients to develop an inventory of self-inferiority beliefs (e.g., "I believe I am too fat; I believe I am not smart enough; I believe I am not far enough along in my career, etc.). In such inventories, what is left out can be as significant as what is included in terms of shame identification.

Kaufman (1985, p. 87) notes that withdrawal is a major defensive strategy employed by people against a shame experience. For individuals with BPD such a defensive strategy could produce a dual diagnosis state. Schizoid Personality

Disorder or Avoidant Personality Disorder are two possible diagnostic conditions that could emanate from the use of a withdrawal strategy to manage shame. The withdrawal likely would include a mixture of psychological and social withdrawal. In order for the withdrawal strategy to work, denial of the shame experience or its impact seem crucial.

Individuals employ a range of withdrawal strategies which includes physical, cognitive, emotional, interpersonal, and social withdrawal. From a clinical perspective withdrawal pertains to varying styles of defensive strategy. Similarly, denial is understood clinically as a dimensional concept rather than a categorical concept. In my clinical work with borderline clients, I have noticed denial employed by BPD clients that differs in degree. I do not wish to suggest that borderline clients use of denial is in any way unique to them. Rather, it seems that denial is quite central to their overall manner of coping.

The mildest form of denial is a *denial of awareness*. This level of denial is differentiated from lying by clients believing what they say. Denying that a subsequent therapy session had been scheduled when it is clearly written on the therapist's scheduling book my be an example of denial of awareness.

A second level of denial is *denial of meaning*. At this level of denial BPD clients deny any other meaning to a situation or to their behavior except for the meaning they hold. Borderline clients often deny that self-destructive behaviors have any meaning relative to poor self-identity or low self-esteem. For them such behaviors often are limited to them simply wanting to do the behaviors, while denying or ridiculing any deeper meanings. It is at this level of denial that the close relationship between splitting, denial, and projective identification can be seen.

A third level of denial is *denial of consequences*. At this level of denial BPD clients deny responsibility for the negative consequences. The denial can take several forms—denying the meaning, denying personal accountability, or projecting the consequences elsewhere. Denying that cutting your wrists has any long term negative consequences, as long as the cuts are not too deep, is an example of this type of denial.

The most florid level of denial is *denial of occurrence*. Borderline clients who deny they were physically abused as a child, even when there are substantiating child welfare records that they are shown, are engaging in this form of denial. It is obviously a clinical judgment call when denial crosses over into unconscious distortion and when apparently unconscious material is actually being denied.

REFERENCES

Bradshaw, J. (1988). *Healing the shame that binds you.* Deerfield Beach, FL: Health Communications, Inc.

Kaufman, G. (1985). *Shame.* Cambridge, MA: Schenkman Publishing Co.

Kaufman, G. (1989). *The psychology of shame.* New York: Springer Publishing Co.

Lewis, H. B. (1987). Shame and the narcissistic personality. In D. L. Nathanson (Ed.), *The many faces of shame.* New York: The Guilford Press.

Lewis, H. B. (1971). Shame and guilt in neurosis. New York: International Universities Press, Inc.

Mahler, M. S. (1971). A study of the separation-individuation process. *The Psychoanalytic Study of the Child, 26,* 403–424.

Morrison, A. P. (1989). *Shame: The underside of narcissism.* Hillsdale, NJ: The Analytic Press.

Tomkins, S. S. (1987). Shame. In D. L. Nathanson (Ed.), *The many faces of shame.* New York: The Guilford Press.

Wurmser, L. (1987). Shame: The veiled companion of narcissism. In D. L. Nathanson (Ed.), *The many faces of shame.* New York: The Guilford Press.

Psychotherapy Approaches with Borderline Clients

4

As noted previously the "borderline" diagnostic category has its origins and clinical influences in traditional psychoanalytic thought. Understandably, the vast majority of professional literature on BPD bears a heavy psychoanalytic influence.

The literature on BPD expanded greatly as the Object Relations School grew in importance in the United States during the 1970s and 1980s. This modern version of psychoanalytic theory sought to describe how psychological meaning develops in infants and toddlers, how the self develops from emotionally significant interactions with caregivers, and how emotions become associated with and expressed through the self.

Although a modern version of psychoanalysis, Object Relations (OR) theory retains many of the strengths and weaknesses of traditional psychoanalytic thought. OR theory attempts to describe how inner psychological meaning and the self develop in infants and toddlers. The matrix for this description is the mother-infant interaction. OR theory describes how infants evolve from a symbiotic extension of the mothering figure to develop their own identity through a series of separating and independence-enhancing behaviors. OR theory is a critical phase theory of child development. It presumes that if particular developmental tasks are not accomplished during a specific chronological age, the young child will suffer predictable and possibly severe psychological damage. An example of a developmental task within a critical phase is a toddler in the 18 to 36 month age range who is learning and being reinforced by the mother to be separated comfortably from the mothering figure. Failure to develop this skill by age 3, according to OR theory, can be one of the causes of borderline personality disorder.

A major gap in OR theory is its lack of a social psychological perspective. OR theory ignores the material environment of a toddler, along with ignoring the extra-family social milieu as developmental influences on young children. An example of extra-family social milieu would be a day-care center. More and more infants are being exposed to day care environments during their pre-oedipal period of development. In psychoanalytic thought BPD is a pre-oedipal disorder that develops during the first 3 years of life and then lies dormant until adolescence or early adulthood. As a consequence, the psychoanalytic, OR, and self psychology perspectives on BPD that are summarized in this chapter all share a serious common limitation. Each of these perspectives is limited to an intrapsychic explanation of BPD. While each perspective focuses on child-caregiver relationships, the theoretical focus is on the intrapsychic consequences to the toddler of these formative relationships.

JAMES MASTERSON'S BPD THEORY OF MATERNAL LIBIDINAL UNAVAILABILITY

Masterson (1981) is the most vocal advocate of the thesis that individuals with BPD have been raised by borderline mothers. While he advocated this thesis absolutely in the early 1970s, he has moderated his position with time. He now acknowledges that other mother factors, albeit also pathological, besides her BPD can produce BPD in her child (Masterson, 1981).

Masterson is also the strongest proponent of pinpointing the developmental origins of BPD within the rapprochement subphase of the initial separation-individuation process (Meissner, 1988, p. 88). He believes that by age 3 the developmental arrests necessary to produce BPD already have occurred. He sees no developmental experiences that can reverse or neutralize the BPD-inducing developmental arrests of the separation-individuation period.

Masterson's BPD theory considers that:

> the core borderline pathology ... is the abandonment depression that results from the failure to resolve the rapprochement crisis. This developmental arrest and the associated failure to achieve object constancy impair the individual's ability to relate to separate objects, subject the vicissitudes of object relationships to the individual's varying need states, create a defect on the capacity of evocative memory, and impede the ability to mourn. Any object loss or separation becomes a catastrophe, which reactivates the intense abandonment depression. (Meissner, 1988, pp. 88–89)

The most noticeable behavioral changes that occur during the separation-individuation phase with toddlers are the onset of walking and talking. It is primarily through locomotion (separation) and communication (individuation) that self development accelerates during this growth period. The fixed enduring nature of psychological damage associated with presumed developmental difficulties during this 18–48 month period has been treated by all of psychoanalysis as an ideological fact, not a scientific empirical fact. The advances of separation and individuation that occur with the onset of walking and speech create tension in the relationship between the toddler and adult caregiver around the struggle of dependency versus autonomy. Presumably, if this tension is not balanced well, BPD can be an outcome.

Masterson's theory is a developmental object relations theory. Four of his core concepts are two-part self images—an all-good self image and an all-bad self image—and two part object (or significant other) images, one that is all good and one that is all bad. According to Masterson, if a toddler successfully develops the skills of the rapprochement crisis, he/she develops an integrated self image and an integrated other image. It is with the presence of these images that "all or none" perceptions give way to more balanced perceptions that include a mix of positive and negative features. The early development of this integrated whole self image or object constancy, that includes self-esteem, occurs for the most part through the achievement of using self-assertion to identify and to activate in reality the toddler's own individuative thoughts, wishes, and feelings (Masterson, 1981).

Masterson sees the difficulties that borderline clients have with self-expression versus false self or defensive expression as due to their need to avoid identifying and activating individuated thoughts and wishes in order to defend against the abandonment depression such authentic expression could trigger (Masterson, 1981). This abandonment is the result of the mother withdrawing her support while the toddler was learning new autonomies.

Masterson refers to the negative part self image as the withdrawing object relations unit (WORU). This unit arises from interactions with the mother during the pre-oedipal period (first 3 or 4 years of life) when punishment occurred to the toddler for spontaneous, self-expression. This part unit becomes part of the borderline person's false self (Masterson, 1981).

According to Masterson, the positive part self image arises from the alliance of the rewarding object relations unit (RORU) and the toddler's pathological or symbiotic ego, which is largely made up of the caregiver's needs and wishes. This alliance in the toddler becomes the basis for the false self. Thus, Masterson sees individuals with BPD developing a false self consisting of split WORU's and RORU's.

A central task in Masterson's psychoanalytic model is to identify in the here and now and in childhood the borderline triad: avoidance of separation-individuation, abandonment depression, and defensive (false self) coping (Klein, 1989). Confrontation is a major therapeutic technique used to make the split WORU and RORU alliance ego-dystonic by means of confronting the defenses within the borderline triad. Masterson is careful to differentiate confrontation from a countertransferential attack. For him, confrontation means:

> bringing the patient face-to-face with the denied destructive aspects of his behavior and feeling states. . . . It requires that the therapist confront from a neutral, objective, emotional

stance because it is clinically indicated, not out of anger or from his own personal emotional needs, i.e., to be aggressive and assertive, to direct, control or admonish the patient. (Masterson, 1981, p. 136)

Masterson identifies two different types of transferences that borderline clients develop. Each transference calls for a different type of confrontation. The clinging transference calls for the confrontation of the denial of destructive behavior inside or outside of therapy. The distancing transference calls for the confrontation of negative hostile projections, usually on the therapist. As Masterson notes:

> The confrontation, when taken in and integrated by the patient, overcomes the avoidance and denial and creates a conflict where none had previously existed. The patient now perceives the destructiveness of his behavior, and although he is tempted to continue it to relieve his abandonment depression, he recognizes that he cannot do so without being harmful to himself. This interrupts the operation of the borderline triad and leads him to control the behavior, which then activates the WORU, which in turn activates again the RORU as resistance. There results a circular process, sequentially including resistance, confrontation, working-through of the feelings of abandonment (withdrawing part-unit), further resistance (rewarding part-unit) and further confrontation, which leads in turn to further working-through. Finally, a more or less continuous activation of the WORU occurs as the focus of the therapy concentrates through fantasies, dreams, memories and painful affects [anxiety and depression] on working-through the patient's depression at separation from mother. (1981, p. 137)

Masterson offers two types of psychoanalytic psychotherapy to borderline clients—confrontive and reconstructive. According to Chatham (1989, p. 344). Masterson considers confrontive psychotherapy to be in order during the early phases of therapy (presumably for all borderline clients). This form of psychotherapy is also called for if therapy occurs once a week or if there are time limits on how long the therapy can last.

For Masterson the goal of confrontive psychotherapy "is to help the patients gain control over acting out and to find appropriate sublimations for the abandonment depression (e.g., jogging)" (Chatham, 1989, p. 344). In terms of how confrontive psychotherapy is conducted, Masterson takes the traditional psychoanalytic position that the therapist's technical neutrality should not be compromised. Technical neutrality refers to the therapist remaining emotionally objective and giving clients no assistance in problem solving (Chatham, 1989, p. 345).

Confrontation, for Masterson, does not mean direct and aggressive challenging. For him:

> confrontations can be statements given firmly but supportively or questions that imply an answer. . . . at no time is the confrontation meant to be harsh or aggressive; instead, it must be made from the position of being on the patient's side and with gentleness, tact and firmness. (Chatham, 1989, p. 345)

Masterson notes that confrontive psychotherapy can be used by clinicians not trained or committed to a psychoanalytic approach to psychotherapy (Chatham, 1989, p. 346). Masterson describes three phases of confrontive psychotherapy. The first involves borderline clients testing their therapists; this phase may last for months or for years. The following quote suggests some iatrogenic assumptions by therapists working with the Masterson model that could be quite disruptive to therapy:

> Masterson has noted that borderline patients, by definition, enter therapy with a great deal of resistance. [For borderline clients] the repetition compulsion . . . is not to master conflict, as with the neurotic, but rather to avoid separation anxiety and abandonment depression. Borderline patients do not want to give up the only strategy they have for controlling these painful affects; thus they deny the destructive aspects of their acting out. Convincing the patients of the destructiveness of their acting out is the hardest task the therapist faces. Complicating this task is the fact that borderline patients do not have the capacity to experience a therapeutic alliance because they lack whole-object relations, and so they relate in therapy by acting out. (Chatham, 1989, p. 346)

Masterson's comments about borderline patients entering therapy with a good deal of resistance and lacking the capacity to experience a therapeutic alliance suggest he is focusing on the more severely impaired borderline client. As with every borderline feature there is great diversity in the severity of borderline symptoms. Masterson's descriptions may be more apropos to inpatient than to outpatient borderline populations.

The second phase of therapy, according to Masterson, begins when the acting out is under control. This phase equates with reconstructive psychotherapy and its goal is to work through the abandonment depression which has become more obvious with the removal of the mask of acting out. Chatham (1989, pp. 349–350) identifies the following helpful therapeutic forces during this phase of therapy: the reliability of the therapist; the therapeutic relationship itself; and the activities of the therapist that include listening, confrontation, interpretation and communicative matching. These activities are intended to address the client's abandonment depression by simultaneously meeting dependency needs while encouraging the client to individuate.

Phase three of therapy is simply the successful working through of abandonment depression and more effective living in all major areas of patients' lives (Chatham, 1989). In Masterson's terms the working through of conflict in the patient requires addressing the split between the patient's withdrawing object relations part-unit (WORU) and the rewarding object relations part-unit (RORU). Such working through is accomplished by a series of confrontations, interpretations, and therapeutic reframing (Masterson, 1981, pp. 168–182).

OTTO KERNBERG AND BORDERLINE PERSONALITY ORGANIZATION

Kernberg's writing on borderline personality organization (BPO) has had enormous influence on the clinical field. However, it is important to recognize that BPO and BPD have in no way the same referent. Kernberg's (1967) theories about BPO were formed in the 1960s from a traditional instinct-oriented psychoanalytic framework. With the publications of Diagnostic and Statistical Manuals III and III-R in 1980 and 1987, respectively, the psychiatric field diverged greatly from Kernberg's perspective. For Kernberg, BPO has continued to be an underlying type of generic personality organization on par with psychosis and neurosis. As such, BPO is a much broader concept than is BPD. With the development in 1980 of BPD as an officially recognized psychiatric diagnosis, several things occurred. First, Kernberg's BPO concept lost much of its usefulness to the general psychiatric practice community. Second, a documented diagnosis of "borderline" by non-psychoanalytic trained clinicians became possible. Third, for the first time since its origin in the 1930s, the "borderline" concept was shaped by non-psychoanalytic content. Kroll (1988) has provided a brief history of this psychoanalytic defrocking of the "borderline" concept. Nonetheless, elements of Kernberg's orthodox conception of BPO continue to influence clinicians' conceptions of individuals with BPD. Kernberg (1967, pp. 641–642) drove the final nail in the lingering debate of where the borderline state stood in reference to neurotic and psychotic states. He clearly differentiated the three psychopathological states by viewing individuals with borderline constellations as having ego structures which could be differentially diagnosed from either neurotic or psychotic states. This distinction constitutes a major contribution.

In making the differentiation of these three states, Kernberg (1967, pp. 661–662) focused on the strengths and weaknesses of the ego structure of each state. He described three nonspecific ego weaknesses in the borderline state: very limited anxiety tolerance; very poor impulse control; and poorly developed sublimatory channels that severely limit creative enjoyment and creative achievement.

He also identified specific ego weaknesses. For him splitting is the central ego defensive operation that is the defining feature of BPO. Kernberg uses "splitting" in a very restricted sense to mean:

> the active process of keeping apart introjections and identifications of opposite quality . . . . The direct clinical manifestation of splitting may be the alternative expression of complementary sides of a conflict . . . combined with bland denial and

lack of concern over the contradiction in his behavior and internal experience of the patient. (1967, p. 667)

Despite Kernberg's acknowledgment that his concept of "splitting" was very restrictive, it seems to remain the dominant concept of splitting employed by clinicians today. In the quote that follows, it is Kernberg who identifies splitting as an infantile-only primitive ego defense mechanism:

Introjections and identifications established under the influence of libidinal drive derivatives are at first built up separately from those established under the influence of aggressive drive derivatives. . . . This division of internalized object relations into 'good' and 'bad' happens at first simply because of the lack of integrative capacity of the early ego. Later on, what originally was a lack of integrative capacity is used defensively by the emerging ego in order to prevent the generalization of anxiety and to protect the ego core built around positive introjections. . . . *This defensive division of the ego, in which what was at first a simple defect in integration is then used actively for other purposes, is in essence the mechanism of splitting.* This mechanism is normally used only in an early stage of ego development during the first year of life, and rapidly is replaced by higher level defensive operations of the ego which center around repression and related mechanisms such as reaction formation, isolation and undoing. . . . Splitting protects the ego from conflicts by means of the dissociation or active maintaining apart of introjections and identifications of [a] strongly conflictual nature. . . (1967, pp. 663–664)

For Kernberg one of the ongoing functions of splitting for borderline individuals is to help them avoid anxiety. Both sides of a split experience (e.g., love and anger towards one's spouse) can be accessed. The problem is that Kernberg believes borderline individuals must access these contradictory states sequentially rather than have the ability to experience both states simultaneously.

Kernberg's therapeutic approach with borderline clients is very much the approach of traditional psychoanalysis, with some minor modifications. Eva Goldstein describes the following structure in Kernberg's expressive psychotherapy with borderline clients:

(1) the patient sits up and faces the therapist rather than lies on a couch; (2) the psychotherapy sessions take place a minimum of two times a week, although three weekly meetings are more optimal initially and more frequent sessions may be helpful later; (3) the therapist adheres to a fixed schedule of appointment times for specified intervals and is clear about policies regarding cancellations and missed sessions; (4) the therapist focuses on the patient's current life situations and relationships, particularly early in treatment; (5) the therapist sets limits on the patient's acting-out within the sessions as reflected in extremely provocative or aggressive behavior, demands on the therapist for extra time, personal information, involvement in the patient's life or need gratification; (6) the patient's life is sufficiently structured, through hospitalization or other means, so that destructive impulses and behavior are not permitted to disrupt the treatment. (Goldstein, 1990, p. 104)

There should be no doubt about the importance of therapeutic intensity in Kernberg's model. As Goldstein (1990, p. 104) notes, Kernberg "regards once a week treatment as problematic in that it usually results in a therapist's excessive preoccupation with the patient's life between sessions. This makes the use of an interpretative approach more difficult".

As William Goldstein (1985) notes about the Kernberg model, the therapist's clinical neutrality is maintained to the extent possible. Interpretation and confrontation are the primary therapy techniques used while the main therapeutic focus is on selected aspects of the transference phenomenon. Because of the decompensation possibilities, the therapeutic focus on a particular transference issue is rapid and remains in the here and now. In the following quote Goldstein describes Kernberg's interpretative approach to transference issues:

There is a basic strategy of interpreting the negative transference and the primitive aspects of the positive transference while 'respecting' those aspects of the positive transference that gradually foster the development of the therapeutic alliance. Negative transferences are systematically elaborated initially only in the here and now, without psychogenetic reconstructions. (1985, p. 207)

Kernberg, like Masterson, sees borderline conditions as occurring during the pre-oedipal period of development. Kernberg assumes that borderline clients have accumulated an excess of instinctual-based aggression due to the prevalence of splitting. One of Kernberg's goals is to metabolize the accumulated aggression via interpretation so that a psychic block to further growth is dissolved within the client.

Kernberg offers two types of psychotherapy for borderline clients—expressive and supportive. According to Chatham (1989, p. 334), "expressive psychotherapy requires a minimum of two sessions per week, preferably three or more. . . . The goal of this therapy is integration of the split-object-relations unit . . . resulting in the capacity to work, love and play."

Expressive psychotherapy is conducted with clinician and client sitting face to face. Technical neutrality, interpreting but not intervening in client behavior, is a central therapeutic principle in Kernberg's approach with borderline clients. Technical neutrality is a central organizing force in expressive psychotherapy (Chatham, 1989, p. 334). Goldstein (1990, p. 107) describes technical neutrality as requiring the therapist not to align with the client's id, ego or superego activities. In addition to remaining objective, therapists must be neutral in another sense—they are not to gratify clients through transference activities. Rather, they are to help clients explore and understand what the therapeutic relationship means rather than letting it be a gratification end in itself.

Technical neutrality is violated any time the clinician must intervene in the client's life, such as taking suicide precautions on behalf of the client. Technical neutrality also is violated when the clinician affirms or acknowledges gains or accomplishments achieved in the client's therapy or personal life. According to Kernberg it is imperative that the clinician reestablish technical neutrality in the therapeutic relationship whenever it has been compromised.

With technical neutrality as a framework, there are four major therapeutic techniques used in expressive psychotherapy: clarification, confrontation, interpretation, and transference analysis. Clarification is used most in the early phases of expressive psychotherapy (Chatham, 1989, p. 336). According to Goldstein (1990, pp. 110–111) clarification in therapy is a cognitive process designed to help the therapist understand the client. It is used when client material is confusing, contradictory, or seemingly distorted. Clarification also is used to determine clients' level of self-awareness and awareness of the implications of their behaviors and current circumstances.

There are no requirements restricting clarification to the early phases of therapy. In the natural progression of the therapeutic alliance, there is less need for clarification as the empathic connection improves between clinician and client.

Confrontation is a second important technique used in expressive psychotherapy. Chatham (1989, p. 336) describes confrontation as "the process of tactfully and subtly pointing out the internal contradictions of the patient's material after it has been clarified." The major function of confrontation is to produce object constancy integrating the split object relations (all or none) categories so prominent in borderline psychology. Increased awareness and helping clients reframe the meaning of their thoughts, feelings, and behaviors are two ways by which confrontation fulfills its function (Chatham, 1989, p. 336). Confrontation usually brings the clinician and client into direct opposition with the defense mechanisms borderline clients employ to keep hurtful material split off from awareness or full understanding. It is important, however, to realize that confrontation will not necessarily activate the acting out scenarios made infamous by so many psychoanalytic writers when describing borderline clients.

After the early phases of expressive psychotherapy, interpretation becomes the main therapeutic technique (Chatham, 1989, p. 336). Interpretation can focus either on the here and now or on the client's childhood and past adult experiences. Goldstein offers the following:

> . . . [interpretation] involves presenting patients with possible explanations of the underlying motives for their defenses, transference reactions, or other self-destructive and self-defeating behavior. Such interpretations have an ego strengthening effect on borderline patients. The therapist usually interprets dominant themes in the sessions, works from surface to depth in the sense that material closer to consciousness is in-

terpreted before unconscious material, addresses the patient's lack of awareness of significant feelings, and comments on the conflictual aspects of the patient's thoughts, feelings and behavior. (1989, pp. 112–113)

The major content focus of expressive psychotherapy is on analyzing the client's transference. According to Chatham this analysis can be done by using the following approach:

1. Negative transference should be explored in the here and now.
2. Moderate aspects of idealization of the therapist can be left alone (e.g., patients compliment therapist about being smart) in order to foster a therapeutic alliance. Extreme idealization must be dealt with because Kernberg believes it represents one-half of a split-off paranoid projection.
3. Systematic interpretation of primitive defenses, even when they are not demonstrating transference, is crucial.
4. Blocking of acting out within and outside the session is important. When outside the session, this should be done by a team member other than the therapist.
5. The therapist must clarify the patients' perceptions before interpreting severe regression in the transference. The therapist and the patient must maintain a 'common boundary of reality'.
6. Magical use of the therapist's interpretation must, in turn, be interpreted (e.g., 'the fact that you are talking with me means you love me' . . .)
7. Destructive sexual acting out must be disentangled from sexual exploration, particularly with adolescents. (1989, p. 337)

Kernberg believes that therapists should not share their countertransference issues with clients because to do so violates technical neutrality. He also believes that extended silences in sessions are counterproductive. Questions and/or interpretations of silence are two ways to get the therapy session moving. Interestingly, Kernberg believes therapists can employ projective identification to help impose order on clients' chaotic psychologies or lifestyles. The use of projective identification is done through interpretation (Chatham, 1989).

The second type of psychotherapy Kernberg offers for borderline clients is called supportive. According to Chatham (1989, p. 340) supportive psychotherapy is a "watered down" version of expressive psychotherapy. Supportive psychotherapy is deemed appropriate for very low functioning borderline clients and is offered to clients once a week or less.

However, according to Kernberg, the goals of supportive psychotherapy should be broader and richer. He proposes focusing psychotherapy on clients' borderline personality defenses and helping them to see the counterproductive consequences that flow from the use of these defenses (1989, p. 340).

From a technique perspective, perhaps the biggest difference between expressive and supportive psychotherapy is the absence of technical neutrality in the latter. Chatham describes supportive psychotherapy:

> The techniques of supportive psychotherapy, according to Kernberg, are suggestion, environmental intervention, clarification, and at times *abreactment*, . . . Supportive psychotherapy does not use interpretation. The therapist may directly express support through cognitive means (e.g., suggestion, persuasion, advice and information) as well as affective means (e.g. praise). All of these techniques, in effect, eliminate technical neutrality. Finally, the therapist does not work with transference. . . . (Chatham, 1989, p. 340)

Supportive psychotherapy usually occurs with weekly or every other week sessions. Chatham (1989, p. 340) lists the conditions and criteria for when borderline clients should receive Kernberg's supportive psychotherapy. The list includes severely acting out clients and those who lack the resources (e.g., motivation, finances, time, recurring crises in daily life) for more intensive psychotherapy. Supportive psychotherapy also is called for if the client is currently receiving secondary gain in their existing circumstances, if severe anti-social behavior is present, or if clients have very limited anxiety tolerance, poor impulse control, or limited skills in creative enjoyment or creative achievement.

In supportive psychotherapy, therapist and patient sit face to face. One problem area in the patient's life is agreed upon for therapeutic focus. Supportive psychotherapy can continue indefinitely with sessions occurring in frequency in direct proportion to patients' serenity and order in their lives.

A review of Kernberg's writings suggest that he may have formulated his treatment ideas for borderline patients from working with the hospitalized or more severe type of borderline patient. However, for therapeutic purposes he does not seem to recognize the dimensional aspect of the borderline condition. Non-hospitalized clients with BPD present clinically very differently in therapy than do hospitalized clients with BPD.

HEINZ KOHUT'S BORDERLINE THEORY OF SELF PSYCHOLOGY

In order to understand Kohut's approach to BPD, it is necessary to understand his theory of self psychology which he developed with Ernest Wolf. Kohut's work is a major reconceptualization of Freud's psychoanalysis (Wolf, 1988). Two concepts central to Kohut's theory are "self" and "selfobject."

As noted in Chapter 2 Kohut considers the self as the individual's psychological core. The continuity, stability, purpose, and meaning in daily living that individuals experience Kohut attributes directly to the degree of self development in the individual. It is through self development that individuals develop the skills to initiate, and to express their ambitions, ideals, and talents. It is through the self that individuals are capable of becoming self-directed and self-sustaining (Wolf, 1988, p. 182).

Kohut theorizes that self development occurs through selfobject experiences. For Kohut, the selfobject aspect of experiences represents the subjective or intrapsychic impact on individuals of their experiences (Wolf, 1982, p. 52). It is for this reason that two siblings never have the same parental experiences. The subjective impact of a parent's praise or disapproval on one child can be very different than an apparently similar parental behavior with the other child.

As Goldstein notes, Kohut and Wolf identified six types of self object experiences that shape a young child's self.

> Kohut . . . identified three main types of selfobject needs in the child's early environment: the need for mirroring that confirms the child's sense of vigor, greatness and perfection; the need for an idealization of other whose strength and calmness soothe the child; and the need for a twin or alter-ego who provides the child with a sense of humanness, likeness to, and partnership with others. (1990, p. 70)

In an apparent extension of Kohut's work, Wolf identified three additional developmental selfobject needs that initially shape the self: the need for merger experiences, the need for an adversary, and the need for efficacy. For Wolf the selfobject need of merging is simply another way of describing the early strivings for symbiosis of young children. Wolf's selfobject need for an adversary seems to be the child's beginning efforts at autonomy and the tensions of connectedness and separation that go with such strivings. Wolf's selfobject need for efficacy appears to be the dawning of the child's sense of competency or empowerment. (1988, p. 55)

Kohut continues a major diagnostic practice begun by classical psychoanalysis. Rather than following the medical model steps of diagnosis, prescription, and treatment, both Kohut and Wolf have dropped the prescription phase and merged the diagnosis and treatment phases for clients they diagnose as borderline. Both make the borderline diagnosis an iatrogenic factor of therapy by using the client's reaction to the therapeutic transference as the major diagnostic indicator. In particular, if the client acts out early and severely in therapy Kohut and Wolf usually diagnose such a client as borderline. It is interesting that both Kohut and Wolf identify the stimulus for the client's "borderline acting out" to be the therapist's faulty therapeutic response. The presumption seems to be that the therapist's faulty response is of some minor nature while the client's reaction is of some major nature

(Wolf, 1988). Thus, continuing a practice begun in the 1930s, "borderline" is defined, in part, through a successful or unsuccessful response to psychoanalytic treatment.

Kohut considers BPD to be a selfobject relations disorder. He avoids connecting the injury that produces the disorder to a particular developmental period. However, he views BPD as arising from permanent injuries to the self that occur early in a person's childhood.

At the clinical level, self-psychology psychotherapy is simply an updated version of psychoanalysis. Despite the use of transference-induced therapeutic regression "the goal of self psychological treatment is to help patients to develop a greater degree of self-cohesion" (Goldstein, 1990, p. 153). Goldstein goes on to note that self-psychology therapy:

> . . . enables patients to reexperience and understand their frustrated selfobject needs for mirroring, idealization and twinship in a new and more empathic context. The therapist immerses himself or herself in the patient's inner world and intervenes in ways that help patients to make sense of their own subjective truth. . . . Enabling patients to 'experience' rather than only 'acquire' knowledge of the self is necessary to the relief of their emotional suffering. . . . Through empathic understanding, optimal frustration, and the repair of disruptions in the selfobject transferences that develop, transmuting internalizations occur that lead to new and stronger self structures [and functions]. (1990, p. 154)

According to Goldstein (1990) self psychotherapy places a great deal of emphasis on therapists' empathic understanding of clients' selfobject needs. These needs in particular include mirroring, idealization, and twinship. Having selfobject experiences within therapy rather than simply acquiring insight is a hallmark of Kohut's therapeutic approach. By generating empathic understanding and creating optimal selfobject frustrations that presumably repair earlier self injuries, clients slowly develop a stronger and clearer self.

The close heritage with psychoanalysis can be seen by the major therapeutic techniques used in self-psychology psychotherapy. Therapists' understanding and explaining, according to Goldstein (1990, p. 164), are the two major therapeutic interventions. Quite simply the therapist's understanding is communicating empathic attunement with the client's subjective reality. Explaining pertains to therapists showing clients linkages between their current behaviors and personalities and the selfobject milieus of the clients' growing-up years. With this intervention, therapy focuses on clients' distorted or missed selfobject experiences rather than focusing on borderline defenses and their dissolution.

For Kohut the occurrence of BPD is not the result of psychological injuries during a specific developmental phase. However, it does seem clear that BPD develops out of selfobject trauma during early childhood. Perhaps Kohut was more empirical and less ideological than were his psychoanalytic predecessors.

Kohut's self-psychology psychotherapy was developed for narcissistic disorders. As a therapeutic medium it is probably appropriate for mild to moderately severe borderline clients.

Self-psychology psychotherapy can be conducted in a face-to-face setting or with the patient lying on a couch. The latter position usually intensifies the therapeutic regression that occurs. For Kohut an empathic therapeutic climate is crucial to effective therapy. He argues against establishing firm therapeutic structure and says therapists need to tolerate "crazy" behavior by their borderline clients (Goldstein, 1990, pp. 154–155).

In lieu of the technical neutrality advocated by both Masterson and Kernberg, Kohut suggests therapists develop an "experience-near-empathy" with their clients. Kohut does not advocate a self-psychology therapeutic approach that is specific to borderline clients. His therapeutic interpretive framework deviates from the psychogenic perspectives taken both by Masterson and Kernberg. Kohut takes an iatrogenic perspective in his approach to therapy and sees that "the patient's reactions in the treatment, even when seemingly irrational, must be understood in relationship to the therapist's characteristics, behavior, or lack of attunement (Goldstein, 1990, p. 155).

It was Kohut's contention that a therapeutic or self-object transference would occur naturally with narcissistically injured patients from the existence of an acceptive and empathic milieu. The issue of whether Kohut's therapy model is more appropriate for narcissistic or borderline personality disordered individuals is probably a non-issue. Clinicians subscribing to Kohut's therapy model have suggested that Kohut's clients who were diagnosed as narcissistic were, in fact, borderline.

Kohut considers the greatest challenge in the early phases of self-psychology therapy to be overcoming the fear of being traumatically injured again, regardless of the diagnosis (Goldstein, 1990, p. 158).

Patients experience self-cohesion—the goal of self-psychology therapy—through the stability of the selfobject transference with the therapist. Paradoxically, it is the disruption of this transference and its immediate repair that helps patients progress. Goldstein describes this process:

> These disruptions (of the transference) must be repaired so that the selfobject transference can be restored. Repeated disruption-repair sequences provide the patient with experiences of 'optimal frustration' that contribute to 'transmuting internalizations' and the development of new self structures. (1990, p. 162)

There is a difference in practice among self-psychology therapists as to the adherence to technical neutrality versus the selective use of mirroring techniques. Wolf (1988, p. 55) defines mirroring techniques as actions by the therapist that meet patients' "need to feel affirmed, confirmed, recognized; to be feeling accepted and appreciated, especially when able to show oneself." Goldstein highlights this split among this school of therapists:

> Many self psychologists take the position that psychoanalytic treatment should confine itself to understanding and explaining patients' selfobject needs rather than gratifying them. Some self psychological therapists believe that selectively providing an actual 'mirroring' of the patient's needs for approval, admiration, or affective sharing, or responding to the patient in soothing and other need fulfilling ways, are important techniques particularly in the treatment of those individuals who have been severely deprived of selfobject experiences early in their lives. They argue that the distinction between what is or

is not appropriate to psychoanalysis is arbitrary and has more to do with the lingering reliance on the traditional 'abstinence' model than it does with what is therapeutically indicated. The willingness to use mirroring techniques does necessitate that the practitioner develop a set of criteria for when and with whom to provide mirroring. (1990, pp. 165–166)

Self-psychology therapy has not played a major role in creating new treatment approaches to BPD. Certainly Kohut's belief, not adhered to by some self-psychology therapists, that his therapy was not appropriate for treating BPD is a factor in the limited impact of this therapeutic school. Self psychology's offering of an alternative (use of mirroring techniques) to technical neutrality is a valuable addition to a clinician's range of therapeutic techniques. Perhaps, though, self psychology's most valuable contribution may be philosophical and theoretical. The 19th century influences on classical psychoanalysis are replaced by assumptions more compatible with contemporary clinical and scientific thinking. In addition, the inclusion of the therapist-client dyad as the major analytical focus, in contrast to the traditional psychoanalytic focus on the patient alone, seems closer to the reality of the actual therapy experience.

Kohut's approach is a variant of object relations. Unlike Masterson and Kernberg, Kohut does not specifically limit BPD-inducing injuries to the very early stages of childhood. While the implication is strong that the borderline-inducing injury was in early childhood, Kohut seems not particularly concerned as to when the injury occurred.

AARON BECK'S COGNITIVE THERAPY WITH BPD

The core theoretical and therapeutic concept in Beck's cognitive therapy model is "schema." Until the 1980s cognitive therapy was limited to clients with axis I problems, primarily depression and anxiety. Beck and Freeman (1990, p. 4) define schemas as "the cognitive structures that organize experience and behavior; 'beliefs' and 'rules' represent the content of the schemas and consequently determine the content of the thinking, affect and behavior."

The authors essentially equate "schema" and "personality." Thus, cognitive therapy is seen as quite applicable with all personality-disordered patients. There is a range of schemas from generational, to familial, gender, and geographical, that have a direct impact on personality development (Beck & Freeman, 1990, p. 8).

Beck and Freeman (1990) warn that treating personality-disordered clients can generate a lot of anxiety in these patients. Cognitive therapy uses the definition of "borderline contained in the latest Diagnostic and Statistical Manual." However, as they note, some research shows that in some treatment populations of borderline clients over half have a coexisting axis II diagnosis.

Cognitive therapy does not consider BPD or any of the axis II personality disorders to be self disorders. Rather, personality disorders are considered to be the result of dysfunctional processing of information about the self and other people (Beck & Freeman, 1990). Every person develops their own control system that regulates their impulses. This system operates on the personal beliefs held by the individual (Beck & Freeman, 1990). The authors describe the role of beliefs in cognitive therapy as extremely important. Beliefs are the psychological forces in individuals that personalize the information that make up individual schemas. It is individuals' beliefs that shape behavior and make it uniquely personal (Beck & Freeman, 1990, p. 35).

Beck and Freeman (1990, pp. 35–36) contend that the control system (the system that influences an individual's anticipations and facilitates or inhibits behavior) is very important in personality development. Self-regulation is a particularly important aspect of the control system and operates through the medium of automatic thoughts. It is these thoughts, Beck and Freeman contend, that lead to activities of self-monitoring, self-appraisal and self-evaluation. If automatic thoughts are operating normally to control behaviors and feelings, individuals may not be aware that such thoughts have occurred.

The crux of change in cognitive therapy is built around work with the automatic thoughts of clients. A first step in cognitive therapy is to identify specific automatic thoughts. Automatic thoughts are difficult for individuals to identify precisely because of their automatic or subcortical nature. The second step in working with automatic thoughts is to make believable substitutes for the identified dysfunctional thoughts. The third step is to begin living and feeling the new automatic thoughts. McKay, Davis, and Fanning describe nine characteristics of automatic thoughts:

1. They are specific, discrete messages.
2. Automatic thoughts often appear in shorthand.
3. Automatic thoughts, no matter how irrational, are almost always believed.
4. Automatic thoughts are experienced as spontaneous.
5. Automatic thoughts are often couched in terms of should, ought or must.
6. Automatic thoughts tend to 'awfulize'.
7. Automatic thoughts are relatively idiosyncratic.
8. Automatic thoughts are hard to turn off.
9. Automatic thoughts are learned. (1981, pp. 12–13)

Beck and Freeman recommend against a frontal therapeutic assault on the automatic thoughts of borderline clients. Instead they recommend therapists work with clients via behavior experiments to document the presence of beliefs and opt for gradual, incremental change rather than attempting one step change (1990, p. 205).

Cognitive therapy does not consider BPD a developmental disorder. In cognitive therapy, *when* dysfunctional schemas and beliefs were learned is less important than *how* they became structuralized or repeated enough to become a part of a person's character and thinking process. For categorization purposes, cognitive therapy seems to consider BPD as a comprehensive thought/perception disorder. Rather than labeling such a disorder on the psychotic-neurotic dimension, as has been the classical concern with borderline features, cognitive therapy considers BPD as a disorder in processing information. The perceptual and cognitive distortions are learned and they can be unlearned and changed.

The cognitive schemas or basic assumptions of individuals with BPD play a major role in how they perceive and impose meaning on events as well as how they shape behavior and emotional responses. What seems distinctive about BPD is the relatively large number of distorted schemas. Beck and Freeman (1990, p. 185) quote Jeffrey Young as saying the average number of early maladaptive schemas is 2.5 for non-borderline personality disorders but perhaps as many as 9 for BPD.

Beck and Freeman identify three maladaptive schemas:

> . . . [that] are often uncovered in cognitive therapy with borderline individuals and appear to play a central role in the disorder. These are "The world is dangerous and malevolent," "I am powerless and vulnerable," and "I am inherently unacceptable." (1990, p. 186)

These authors also acknowledge the role of splitting in the cognitive operations of individuals with BPD:

> Borderline individuals can experience the full range of cognitive distortions, but one particular distortion that Beck refers to as 'dichotomous thinking' is particularly common and is particularly problematic. Dichotomous thinking is the tendency to evaluate experiences in terms of mutually exclusive categories . . . rather than seeing experiences as falling along continua. The effect of this 'black-or-white' thinking is to force extreme interpretations on events that would normally fall in the intermediate range of a continuum, since there are no intermediate categories. According to the cognitive view, extreme evaluations of situations lead to extreme emotional responses and extreme actions. (Beck & Freeman, 1990, p. 187)

Beck and Freeman recommend modifying the dichotomous thinking before focusing therapy on "establishing a clearer sense of identity, improving skills at controlling emotions, or changing maladaptive beliefs and assumptions" (1990, p. 189).

In cognitive therapy a task-oriented atmosphere is established as a way to titrate the "transference" aspect of the therapist-client relationship. However, in working with individuals with BPD, much more emphasis than is usual in cognitive therapy is devoted to the therapeutic relationship. A collaborative relationship between the therapist and client is the goal. The initial thrust of cognitive therapy with borderline clients (as it is with all clients) is on concrete behaviors. Such a focus protects clients against the rise of countertherapeutic trust and intimacy issues (Beck & Freeman, 1990, p. 196).

For those not familiar with the techniques used in cognitive therapy, Beck and Freeman list ten such techniques that might be employed with borderline and other personality-disordered clients:

> (1) guided discovery, which enables the patient to recognize stereotyped dysfunctional patterns of interpretation (such as dichotomous thinking); (2) searches for idiosyncratic meaning, since these patients often interpret their experiences in unusual or extreme ways; (3) labeling of inaccurate inferences or distortions, in order to make the patient aware of bias or unreasonableness of particular automatic patterns of thought; (4) collaborative empiricism—working with the patient to test the validity of the patient's beliefs, interpretations, and expectations, (5) examining explanations for other people's behavior; (6) scaling—translating extreme interpretations into dimensional terms to counteract typical dichotomous thinking; (7) reattribution—reassigning responsibility for actions and outcomes; (8) deliberate exaggeration—taking an idea to its extreme which places a situation in high relief and facilitates reevaluation of a dysfunctional conclusion; (9) examining the advantages and disadvantages of maintaining or changing beliefs or behaviors, and clarifying primary and secondary gains; (10) decatastrophizing—enabling the patient to recognize and counter the tendency to think exclusively in terms of the worst possible outcome of a situation. (1990, p. 80)

Juxtaposing the object relations literature on BPD to the cognitive therapy literature on BPD leaves one almost unavoidably with a sense of superficiality about the cognitive therapy model of BPD. Beck and Freeman provided the following translation into cognitive-behavioral terms of the core object relations perspective of BPD:

> ... borderline individual holds extreme, poorly integrated views of relationships with early caregivers and, as a result, holds extreme, unrealistic expectancies regarding interpersonal relationships. These expectancies are seen as consistently shaping both behavior and emotional responses and as

being responsible for the wide range of symptoms these individuals experience. It is assumed by psychodynamic writers that the most appropriate way to resolve this situation is to conduct therapy in such a way that these expectancies will be manifested in the client's relationship with the therapist, where they may be resolved through the application of psychoanalytic techniques in long-term therapy. (1990, p. 183)

Perhaps the best or freshest aspect of cognitive therapy with borderline clients may be a greatly shortened therapy compared to the psychoanalytic approach. As Beck and Freeman (1990, p. 206) note, the time for cognitive therapy with borderline clients is much less than with the traditional psychoanalytic approaches. While the latter are thought to take from 5 to 7 years, cognitive therapy with borderline clients may last only 1½ to 2½ years.

MARSHA LINEHAN'S DIALECTICAL BEHAVIOR THERAPY FOR BPD

This clinically based theory and treatment approach was developed on an outpatient population of female borderline patients. Their most dominant clinical feature was a history of self-mutilating (parasuicidal) behavior.

The use of the term "dialectical" in dialectical behavior therapy (DBT) seems to serve more of an epistemological or an ontological function than it does a theoretical or clinical function. A clinician can become proficient in DBT without truly understanding dialectical logic. In fact, as Linehan uses the term, "dialectics" appears to be a synonym for either "interrelated" or "systemic."

Linehan's theory of BPD is probably less a theory and more an organizing clinical framework. Linehan and Wasson provide the following descriptive matrix of behavioral patterns of BPD:

The behavioral patterns for BPD can be organized along these dialectical poles arranged around a biosocial axis: (1) emotional vulnerability versus invalidation, (2) active passivity versus apparent competence, and (3) unrelenting crisis versus inhibited grieving. Those patterns above the axis (emotional vulnerability, active passivity, unrelenting crisis) are originally most heavily influenced by biological factors associated with emotion regulation. Those patterns below the axis (invalidation, apparent competence, inhibited grieving) are most heavily influenced by social responses to emotional expressiveness. (1990, p. 421)

A real strength in Linehan's model is her consideration of "borderline" as a dimensional term (more than-less than) rather than a categorical (either-or) term. Linehan's clinical approach combines individual therapy with group therapy. Both forms of therapy seem to have a heavy psychoeducation component associated with them. DBT is structured as follows:

> Linehan offers four sequential group treatments: (1) core skills (observing, describing, spontaneously participating, being mindful, being nonjudgmental, and focusing on effectiveness); (2) interpersonal skills; (3) emotion-regulation skills; and (4) distress-tolerance skills. Although the individual therapist has the task of helping the client integrate the skills into daily life, the rudiments of the skills are taught in group sessions. (Linehan & Wasson, 1990, p. 426)

Consistent with a behavior therapy approach treatment goals are organized into clear sequences:

> Treatment targets (goals) in Linehan's therapy are hierarchically arranged as follows: (1) suicidal behaviors (parasuicidal, high risk suicide ideation), (2) behaviors interfering with the conduct of therapy, (3) escape behaviors interfering with a reasonably high quality of life (e.g., substance abuse, poor work behaviors, criminal behaviors, poor judgment), (4) behavioral-skill acquisition (emotion regulation, interpersonal effectiveness, distress tolerance, self-management, (5) other goals the client wants to focus on. (Linehan & Wasson, 1990, p. 426)

DBT has three overriding characteristics. It has a straightforward problem-solving focus, it has an ongoing dialectical format, and it requires the therapist to monitor the client-therapist relationship. According to Linehan and Wasson,

"The overriding dialectic [in DBT] is the necessity of accepting clients just as they are, within a context of trying to teach them to change" (1990, p. 426).

Linehan and Heard (1992) identified five targets of DBT: (1) suicidal and parasuicidal behaviors; (2) therapy-interfering behaviors by either the client or the clinician, (3) life-interfering and escape behaviors, (4) post-traumatic stress reactions and (5) respect for self.

Linehan's dialectical behavior therapy is a radical departure from the traditional theory and therapy of BPD. Consistent with the behaviorist tradition, BPD consists of "the relevant behavioral and associated stimulus content domains" (Linehan & Wasson, 1990, p. 424). Behaviorism does not recognize the existence of a nonbehavioral self. Thus, Linehan's DBT focuses on changing stimulus–response connections that borderline clients have learned. At the therapist–client level DBT seems to involve typical behavior therapy activities (e.g., psychoeducation, documentation, homework, etc.). In addition, DBT seems to place a strong emphasis on a teacher-student type of clinical relationship. Little, if any, therapy time is spent on analyzing the dynamics of the therapeutic relationship. A good deal of responsibility for therapy is given to the client. Between sessions, telephone calls to the therapist are permitted if it is therapeutically warranted. While transference-type analyses are not done in DBT, therapists do use the therapeutic relationship as a contingency management strategy. Simply put, the therapist reminds the client of commitments to therapy made by the client and the therapist is careful to reinforce adaptive client behavior while trying not to reinforce maladaptive behavior. The main focus of DBT is quite clearly on helping clients improve their adjustments and functioning in their personal environment.

As the last two theories and their dates of publication indicate, clinicians trained in specialties other than psychoanalysis are beginning to direct their theoretical attention toward BPD. Clearly, with these new theoretical foci on BPD, there will be a more diversified clinical approach to treating the disorder. A more experimental or open-minded approach to BPD disorder seems long overdue.

REFERENCES

Bandura, A. (1971). Self-efficacy: Towards a unifying theory of behavioral change. *Psychological Review, 84*, 2, pp. 191–215.

Beck, A. T., & Freeman, A. (1990). *Cognitive therapy of personality disorders.* New York: The Guilford Press.

Chatham, P. M. (1989). *Treatment of the borderline personality.* Northvale, NJ: Jason Aronson.

Goldstein, E. G. (1990). *Borderline disorders.* New York: The Guilford Press.

Goldstein, W. N. (1985). *An Introduction to the borderline conditions.* Northlake, NJ: Jason Aronson.

Kernberg, O. (1967). Borderline personality organization. *Journal of the American Psychoanalytic Association, 15*, 641– 685.

Klein, R. (1989). Shorter-term psychotherapy of the personality disorder. In J. F. Masterson & R. Klein (Eds.), *Psychotherapy of the disorders of the self.* New York: Brunner/Mazel.

Kroll, J. (1988). *The challenge of the borderline patient.* New York: W. W. Norton & Co.

Linehan, M. M., & Heard, H. L. (1992). Dialectical behavior therapy for borderline personality disorder. In J. F. Clarkin, E. Marziali, & H. Monroe-Blum (eds.), *Borderline personality disorder: Clinical and empirical perspectives* (pp. 256–258). New York: The Guilford Press.

Linehan, M. H., & Wasson, E. J. (1990). Behavior therapy. In A. S. Bellack & M. Hersen (eds.), *Handbook of comparative treatments for adult disorders* (pp. 420–435). New York: John Wiley & Sons.

Masterson, J. F. (1981). *The narcissistic and borderline disorders.* New York: Brunner/Mazel.

McKay, M., Davis, M., & Fanning, P. (1981). *Thoughts and feelings.* Richmond, CA: New Harbinger Publications.

Meissner, W. W. (1988). *Treatment of patients in the borderline spectrum.* Northvale, NJ: Jason Aronson.

Wolf, E. S. (1988). *Treating the self.* New York: The Guilford Press.

Self-Management Therapy versus Psychoanalytic-Infused Therapy

5

The origins and history of the borderline syndrome are psychoanalytic in nature (Gunderson, 1984, pp. 1–19). A therapy model for BPD that is an alternative to the psychoanalytic approach should delineate clearly those assumptions that are a part of the self-management therapy of BPD. This chapter contrasts the structures of self-management therapy with psychoanalytic-infused therapies. As noted in Chapter 4 there are several psychoanalytic approaches to therapy with borderline clients. Amidst these variations there are core features that are a part of psychoanalytic-influenced therapy. This chapter examines 11 features that differentiate self-management therapy of BPD from the traditional therapeutic approach to working with borderline clients.

SELF-MANAGEMENT THEORY OF BPD

Self-management theory identifies BPD as primarily a disorder of the self. The therapeutic objective in this clinical approach to BPD is not to help the client achieve object constancy as it is in psychoanalytic-influenced therapy. Rather, the goal is to enhance the development of self-efficacy. Self-efficacy refers to a person's belief that specific behavior will achieve a particular goal and the person can perform the behavior well enough to attain that goal. It should be noted that

117

self-efficacy was one of the selfobject needs identified by Wolf in the Kohutian self psychology therapy model. The development of self-efficacy is an evolving lifelong process and is in no way age or stage specific.

As described by Bandura, self-efficacy has two central dimensions—outcome expectations and efficacy or competence expectations. Bandura describes these two sets of expectations:

> An outcome expectancy is defined as a person's estimate that a given behavior will lead to certain outcomes. An efficacy expectations is the conviction that one can successfully execute the behavior required to produce the outcomes. Outcome and efficacy expectations are differentiated because individuals can believe that a particular course of action will produce certain outcomes, but if they entertain serious doubts about whether they can perform the necessary activities such information does not influence their behavior . . . expectations of personal mastery affect both initiation and persistence of coping behavior. The strength of people's convictions in their own effectiveness is likely to affect whether they will even try to cope with given situations. . . . Efficacy expectations determine how much effort people will expend and how long they will persist in the face of obstacles and aversive experiences. The stronger the perceived self-efficacy, the more active the efforts. (1977, pp. 193–194)

Thus, self-efficacy is a cognitive concept that links the self-function to behavior. Self-efficacy is one of the many self-functions impaired by BPD.

Self-management theory is not a theory of BPD causation. Rather, it is a theory of clinical intervention. It breaks from the psychoanalytic tradition by viewing BPD as a trauma-based disorder, not a developmental disorder. The combination of trauma, plus inadequate or unstable self-functions, are the core conditions leading to BPD. Self-management theory does not make a critical stage or particular age assumption of when the trauma occurred or the self became disordered. At this stage of our clinical and scientific knowledge, it is not possible to determine the temporal sequencing of the occurrence of psychological trauma and the self disorder with people diagnosed with BPD. The trauma is severe enough to generate a post-traumatic stress disorder in the individual. This disorder often goes unrecognized and untreated under classical (psychoanalytic) clinical assumptions.

Self-management therapy considers toxic shame to be the core disabling emotion of BPD. Psychoanalytic thought always has identified excessive aggression as a central therapeutic feature of BPD. Shame is a psychological force that helps shape both the self and personal identity. As a psychological force shame can split the self or align with the split selves. In individuals with BPD, a major therapeutic goal of self-management therapy is to teach them to recognize, to label, and to manage their toxic shame. Shame is seen as blocking or eroding the impact of self-efficacy.

Self-management therapy is an amalgam of psychodynamic, cognitive, and behavioral therapies of BPD. (Table 5.1 contains a summary of self-management therapy.) While rejecting the psychodynamic causative model, self-management theory accepts the central role that splitting and projective identification play in the psychology and interpersonal styles of individuals with BPD. While rejecting the cognitive theory of BPD—faulty processing of information—self-management accepts the mediating role in behavior played by the self-efficacy function. While rejecting the behavioral concept of BPD, self-management therapy accepts the role homework plays in self-management therapy for individuals with BPD. Self-management therapy uses concrete targeted homework as one way of integrating therapy into the daily lives of borderline clients.

Self-management therapy promotes self-efficacy through using psychoeducation, homework, and a therapeutic partner relationship to develop inner direction and appropriately assertive behavior for clients with BPD. A moderate to mild level of emotional intensity is maintained during therapy sessions so as not to engender passivity or regression in the client. Because of the prevalence of splitting by clients with BPD, self-management therapy makes the lifestyles of borderline clients a therapeutic focus. Self-management therapy re-

TABLE 5.1 Summary of Self-Management Therapy of Borderline Personality Disorder

Event	Consequence	Intervention
Trauma	Post-traumatic stress disorder	Identify, integrate.
Failed autonomy (inadequate experience in independence)	Shame	Recognize, label, and manage shame.
	Damaged self-efficacy	Improve outcome expectancy. Improve efficacy expectancy.
Identify diffusion (inadequate experience in individual expression)	Possible addictions	Recovery program.
	Abandonment panic	Psychoeducation. Social support network.
	Emotional instability	Possible medication. Analysis and change of self-talk.

jects the therapeutic principle of technical neutrality as inappropriate for clients with BPD. Very often the trauma experienced by individuals with BPD is both unrecognized and unlabeled. With many borderline clients, the objective dimensions of the trauma do not appear "that bad." However, it is imperative to remember that the psychological damage inflicted by a post-traumatic stress disorder results as much from the subjective meaning the stressor event has for the individual as does the stressor event per se.

Because of the psychodynamics that are such a central part of BPD (splitting, avoidance, denial, rigidity, fear of change, shame, etc.), therapeutic change is a combination of insight, behavioral change, and lifestyle change. Also, because of these same psychodynamics, self-management therapy involves a lot of repetition.

Splitting is an active process that impacts each therapy session. As a consequence an insight or a particular behavioral or lifestyle change often is eroded by the impact of splitting or some other psychodynamic process. It is for this reason that a good deal of repetitive clinical work must occur with borderline clients.

An important caveat is in order about the model of self-management therapy for clients with BPD. This model was developed based upon this author's outpatient and inpatient clinical experience with clients diagnosed with BPD and upon his knowledge of the clinical literature. The author rejected the psychoanalytic theory and therapy of BPD for a very simple reason—the theory is neither accurate nor helpful to the client with BPD, nor is the therapy appropriate or reliably helpful to the client.

The following disjuncture in the psychoanalytic or object relations theory of BPD should be remembered. The work of Margaret Mahler that established the stages of child development used by object relations theories of BPD (e.g., normal autism, symbiosis, separation-individuation, on-the-way-to object constancy) was done with presumary normal children and their mothers (Chatham, 1989). The clinical populations that object relations theorists used to develop their theories of BPD were adult borderline patients. In Kernberg's instance the majority of his borderline patients were so severely impaired as to require long-term hospitalization. Thus, the object relations theories of BPD are simply *post hoc* application of child development research findings on adult clinical populations. What has been applied to these populations of borderline adults is orthodox psychoanalytic-influenced object relations theory. In order for such an application to fit, the assumptions must be made that BPD is an early childhood disorder and that borderline adults are and act childlike. Clearly, clinicians making such assumptions do so at their own discretion and peril.

The self-management model considers BPD to be a disorder of the self. Early psychoanalytic theories of BPD considered it to be an ego dysfunction disorder based upon excessive instinctual-based aggression. Later theories, such as Kohut's, viewed BPD as a self disorder that arose out of inadequate social relationship experiences. The cognitive theory of BPD considers the disorder to be the result of perceptual/thought distortions that are based upon faulty learning and faulty self-beliefs. These distortions do not take the form of breaks with reality. Rather, they take the form of schemas that neither break from reality nor accurately portray reality. Linehan's behavior theory of BPD considers the disorder to be due largely to emotional dysregulation. Neither the cognitive theory nor the behavior theory of BPD consider the disorder to be a self disorder.

The dominance of psychoanalytic thought as to the nature of BPD is so complete that it seems important to provide a clear contrast between a psychoanalytic model of BPD and an alternative model, such as the self-management perspective. This perspective acknowledges both a cognitive and a behavioral dimension in the successful clinical intervention of BPD. However, self-management therapy considers the central disorder in BPD to be a disorder of the self.

RECOGNIZE AND PURGE PSYCHOANALYTIC THERAPY ASSUMPTIONS

A focus on the transference part of the therapist-client relationship is the cornerstone of psychoanalytic therapy (Goldstein, 1990, p. 114). Through transference, considered to be the major healing force, the therapist functions as a surrogate parent. The transference is intensified by introducing therapeutic regression in the patient. Such regression induces dependency on the therapist and presumably opens or reveals the patient's developmental injuries to be healed. The focus of change is the ego or the self. The purpose of the therapeutic regression is to overwhelm the primitive and defensive coping techniques (e.g., projection, denial, projective identification) that borderline clients use (Volkan, 1987, p. 57). The therapeutic relationship, which is thought to repeat in many important ways the client's parent–child relationship, then allows the client to relive important emotions in a corrective way.

Self-management therapy seeks to empower borderline clients through increased self-competence. Through psychoeducation and selected changes in lifestyle, clients address one or more of their BPD diagnostic characteristics. The therapy does not focus on the therapist–client emotional relationship, but rather encourages changes in lifestyle and in self skills by the client. Self-management therapy identifies shame and its numerous manifestations in the client's life. Considerable time is spent identifying and working through previously unrecognized or unlabeled post-traumatic stress disorder. If addictions are present, these destructive behaviors must receive therapeutic attention first.

Psychoanalytic therapy treats BPD as a developmental disorder of early childhood. It is seen as a developmental deficit or a developmental fixation due to improper parental caretaking. While not rejecting this perspective, the self-management approach to BPD places much more emphasis on existential trauma as the major cause of BPD. The majority of psychoanalytic theorizing about BPD is based more on ideology than it is on empirical facts. The considerable lag time between the occurrence of the developmental injury (ages 1–4) and the presenting of borderline clients for psychotherapy (usually as young adults) is so great that it is not possible to restrict causative factors to only one developmental phase or to the parent–child relationship.

Mahler's clinical work, which describes the toddler's developmental progression through the various subphases of the separation-individuation phase, represents an important clinical contribution. However, two important points must be realized about Mahler's work and psychoanalytic borderline theory. First, Mahler did not develop her theory from working clinically with borderline individuals. Her clinical data and theory are based upon work with mothers and children. Her work is intended to show interactional differences between mother and child as a function of developmental changes in the very young child between the ages of 5–36 months (Mahler, 1971, p. 405).

Second, none of the major psychoanalytic theorists on the borderline phenomenon based their clinical work on children who became borderline later in life. Instead, adults who were diagnosed with BPD had their "borderlineness" connected by the clinicians deductively to Mahler's formulations. The following quote by Mahler herself indicates how problematic such deductive theorizing is:

> My intention, at first, was to establish in this paper a linking up, in neat detail, of the described substantive issues with specific aspects of borderline phenomena shown by child and adult patients *in the psychoanalytic situation* [my italics]. But I have come to be more and more convinced that there is no 'direct line' from the deductive use of borderline phenomena to one or another substantive finding of observational research. (1971, p. 415)

This quote highlights both the reliability and validity problems associated with connecting adult borderline phenomena with possible early childhood-caretaker interactions. Perhaps even more significant is Mahler's iatrogenic phrase "in the psychoanalytic situation." Her concerns of possible contaminating effects between the current psychoanalytic clinical situation with adult borderline clients and observational research data on children and their mothers should give any thoughtful clinician pause for concern. Clearly, how much the clinician is seeing/interpreting what is biographically accurate for the client and how much represents clinician ideology and projection is a seriously unanswered question. The current inadequacy of theory and therapy for individuals with BPD seems so obvious, yet only recently has the monopolistic approach of psychoanalysis been broken. Relatively untested is the receptivity of the various professional communities of mental health clinicians to new formulations of BPD and nontraditional therapeutic approaches.

THERAPIST LED VERSUS CLIENT LED

In self-management therapy, dialogue replaces free association as the major style of communication. The therapist structures sessions through focused questions. In psychoanalytic-influenced therapy, silence is considered a therapeutic force and the therapist usually takes the role of *not* breaking the silence. In self-management therapy, silences, especially extended silences, are thought to run the danger of generating a shame attack within the client. To insure a clear role, the therapist will ask directly in the early stages of therapy, "How can I help?" To insure reality testing for both the therapist and client during the early sessions, the therapist will ask the client, "What will make this session successful for you?" These therapeutic questions, that are an important part of the early phase of self-management therapy, recognize the limited tolerance—anxiety, anger, frustration, and shame—that characterize borderline clients. In particular, self-management therapy directs specific attention to possible shame triggers in the client which, if activated prematurely, could severely disrupt or terminate therapy. Self-management therapy aims to generate early benefits for borderline clients, albeit perhaps small, as a way to maximize the likelihood of continuing the therapy.

In taking a proactive therapeutic role, the clinician in self-management therapy definitively rejects technical neutrality as a desirable clinician characteristic. In self-management therapy the clinician functions much more as a role model or coach than as a trigger for initiating merging and regressive behaviors on the part of the borderline client. A major deficit for many individuals with BPD includes difficulty initiating and sustaining behavior and it is this difficulty, in part, that clinicians address with their proactive role in therapy. Disruptions in the therapy process usually are considered to be a function of therapy-induced iatrogenic factors rather than a manifestation of client psychogenic factors.

The proactive role of the therapist also serves a psychoeducation function. Self-management therapy does not rely on insight as the major way of producing change in borderline clients. Insight learning frequently is not potent enough to override the splits that shape how such clients learn and use new information. Learning-by-doing is a much more effective learning modality for people with BPD. The therapist as a role model offers clients a much more powerful and immediate learning modality. Impulse control, integrating "either-or" split perspectives, and identifying and managing abandonment feelings probably are accomplished best by client observation and experience with the therapist.

In self-management therapy the therapist-client relationship is not viewed through the veil of transference. Instead,
the therapeutic relationship is seen as a relationship in its
own right. The personality and interpersonal processes active
in the therapeutic relationship get their central meaning from
the participants themselves and are not considered symbolic
of previous relationships. They are not considered to be a repetition of parent-child interactions or the repetition of other
emotionally meaningful relationships. Clearly, clients usually
act in their therapeutic relationship in ways that are consistent with their actions in previous relationships, but such
consistency does not have symbolic therapeutic meaning.
Such consistency simply is an expression of the client's
personality.

PROBLEM SPECIFIC FOCUS VERSUS UNFOCUSED
TOPIC SELECTION

In traditional psychoanalysis free association allows the
client to range over (or avoid) a wide array of topics. Many
therapies let clients start sessions with "wherever they are."
Self-management therapy begins by focusing either on a current crisis in the borderline client's life or on one of the relevant BPD diagnostic characteristics. Keeping clients focused
on a particular problem is one way to speed the therapist's
learning of what meanings clients apply to their experiences.
Due to the cognitive distortions, particularly splitting, borderline clients' meanings for experiences are not always apparent. Since virtually all borderline clients present with
multiple psychiatric problems, there can be a great tempta-
tion, and some justification, for topic-hopping within a session. Such an approach, though, is likely to overwhelm a borderline client whose self boundaries are already porous.

In this same vein, self-management therapy avoids open-
ended questions ("What was your relationship like with your
father?") in favor of more focused questions ("What kind of
fun things did you and your dad do together?"). As self-management therapy progresses, the therapist helps the client see
the interconnections between the various problems focused

on in therapy and BPD, but this more comprehensive focus occurs slowly and occurs later.

For clients prone to recurrent crises, clinicians must balance the therapy time devoted to helping the client solve the crisis with the time devoted to promoting client understanding of the relationship between the recurrent crises and BPD. One important way to promote this understanding is to explore with clients their role in generating or escalating the crises in their lives.

THERAPY INTENSITY MODULATED VERSUS INTENSE TRANSFERENCE ENCOURAGED

As noted in the previous section, borderline clients tend to have poor self boundaries. This limitation makes them vulnerable to diluting their independence in emotionally intense experiences. In self-management therapy it is the therapist's responsibility to set a level of emotional intensity that is compatible with the client's coping skills. Unlike psychoanalytic-influenced therapy, induced regression, and the subsequent dependency on the therapist, is not a desirable therapeutic state. Self-management therapy recognizes that the interpersonal intensity generated in therapy by borderline clients is often simply the result of their idealization/devaluation cycle that is so much a part of BPD. In self-management therapy it is important that therapists anticipate emotionally overwhelming subjects rather than attempt to manage such behaviors via therapeutic interpretation as in psychoanalytic-influenced therapy. In particular, self-management therapy strives for a balance between borderline clients experiencing, recognizing, and labeling shame and being numbed, overwhelmed, and paralyzed by shame. There are some variations of psychoanalysis that intentionally induce a therapy-based psychosis in borderline clients (Volkan, 1987, pp. 93–95).

An important distinction should be drawn between transference-induced intensity and the emotional intensity associated with a post-traumatic stress incident. The former is a controllable iatrogenic artifact of therapy. The latter is a psychogenic factor that is a primary condition of a post-traumatic stress disorder. Very often the abreaction that is a part of healing the psychological damage caused by PTSD is extremely intense. However, the course of intensity that occurs with emotional abreaction of a traumatic experience is just the opposite of the course followed by transference. Usually emotional abreaction peaks quickly and then subsides. Transference-based emotions accumulate slowly and have no apparent discharge schedule or timing.

Client phone calls between sessions to the clinician are appropriate if the client is in some type of crisis. However, if such a practice becomes a regular occurrence, then countertherapeutic dependency on the clinician may have developed. The issue of clinical dependency should be discussed with clients as soon as it appears. On a related issue, in self-management therapy, the use of transitional objects or clinician-substitute objects by clients should be discussed and discouraged. Similarly, clinicians sending clients postcards while on vacation also is countertherapeutic. Instead, vacations or skipped appointments can be opportunities for clients to manage their separation and abandonment issues. Rather than implicitly encouraging client dependency via the use of clinician-substitute transitional objects, clinician absences are anticipated by reviewing with clients their access to a social support network. Therapist dependency undermines the therapeutic goal of client self-efficacy.

CURRENT LIFE FOCUS VERSUS EARLY CHILDHOOD FOCUS

Perhaps the biggest conceptual difference in BPD between self-management therapy and psychoanalysis is that the former does not limit the causation of BPD to the first 3 years of life. Psychoanalytic-influenced therapy uses the major part of therapy time to reconstruct childhood meanings and experiences. Self-management therapy varies with each borderline client. Clients prone to contemporary life crises have a therapy focus much more on the here and now. Borderline clients with considerable trauma in their early years will have therapy focused much more in that period of their lives. Self-management therapy recognizes that borderline clients are helped to change very little by learning the biographical basis of their thoughts, feelings, behaviors, and relationships. Establishing psychological patterns between the borderline clients' past and present holds some interest for self-management therapy. However, identifying such patterns provides little help in how to generate and to manage personal change.

What is important to recognize is that an object relations model of BPD necessarily makes the disorder a childhood developmental one. Obviously, if the borderline injury or deficit is thought to be in childhood, then such a thought will influence the emphasis of therapy.

Self-management therapy advocates a trauma-based model of BPD with no preconceptions of when the trauma occurred. In fact, the assumption is made that the severity and repetitiveness of the trauma are probably more indicative of the subsequent trauma than is the timing of the trauma. Many of the symptoms of BPD are mimicked in PTSD, including the presence of splitting. Many individuals with BPD are not uniformly hampered, for example, in interpersonal relationships. Every client I have worked with on an outpatient basis appeared to be active in at least one nondestructive relationship. If the object relations model of BPD were either comprehensive or accurate, clients with BPD should show no object constancy (Kernberg), constant split object, or all-or-none reactions (Masterson), or no evocative memory (Adler, 1985, pp. 21–27). However, such developmental deficits or fixations show major exceptions with every outpatient borderline client I have seen clinically. The point with individuals with BPD is that they probably do not have a developmental deficit, but rather have a selective or suppressed response capability. This selective response capability may be triggered by the interaction of current stimulus conditions in the context of unresolved trauma. It is important to remember that a major defining consequence of PTSD is the splitting of identity and a major disruption of the trauma victim's response repertoire.

It appears more a function of ideology rather than clinical fact that a characterological disorder such as BPD reflects a pre-oedipal disorder. The fact that every psychoanalytic-influenced clinician must reconcile is that scientific research on child development does not support BPD as a pre-oedipal disorder.

IDENTIFY, DOCUMENT AND LABEL PTSD

The self-management model of BPD considers PTSD an omnipresent aspect of the disorder. However, PTSD is rarely the presenting problem with borderline clients. It is not recognized generally within the community of mental health professionals that PTSD co-occurs with BPD. The cognitive distortions—splitting, projective identification, denial, etc.—coupled with the theoretical belief that borderline-inducing damage occurs in early childhood has helped mask the presence of PTSD (Yule & Williams, 1990, pp. 279–295; Terr, 1989, pp. 3–20; Dyregrov & Mitchell, 1992, pp. 5–17). Adding to this mask is only recent acceptance in mental health treatment circles that children too are susceptible to PTSD. PTSD and its treatment is not an integral part of the psychoanalytic concept and treatment of BPD.

Trauma is a central force in PTSD. Sprinkled throughout the psychoanalytic literature on BPD are references to the consequent trauma to infants and toddlers of non-synchronous behavior toward them by their caretakers. What we have learned in the clinical treatment of PTSD is that the psychological impact of trauma is to split or to tear psychological functions such as self-identity, self-esteem, self-competence, etc. Major characteristics of trauma are sudden, disruptive, harmful, and overwhelming. These characteristics do not seem appropriate for describing developmental trauma, especially as it pertains to child–caregiver interactions. The word "trauma," when referring to developmental misexperiences, seems to lack the pathological splitting that occurs with trauma that induces PTSD. At best, the term "trauma" is simply inaccurate to describe communicative mismatching between parent and toddler.

The core emotion in existential trauma appears to be shame but it is not at all clear that shame is an integral part of developmental "trauma." The presumption that caregivers failed to reinforce borderline clients' efforts to separate and to individuate when the clients were 3 years old or so, and that this failure is traumatic to the young child, seems to fall victim to the categorical logic of psychoanalysis. The reality is probably closer to the fact that caregivers, to greater or lesser degrees, reinforced separation-individuation behaviors of toddlers. The obvious question becomes at what point is the lack of caregiver reinforcement traumatic? A second question is, "With the frequency and diversity of caregivers and the diversity of their responses in today's world of childcare, should not this cacophony of people and styles, with their inevitable missed responses, make us all borderline?" In fact, perhaps no more than 1%–7% of the general population may have BPD. Considering the epidemiological data on child sexual abuse alone, it is not possible that 93%–99% of children in the United States receive "good enough" parenting by their caretakers. So perhaps factors other than parent–child interactions are at play in the occurrence of BPD.

Since PTSD is not essential in establishing a BPD diagnosis, little, if any, attention is devoted to its identification in the early stages of self-management therapy. As experienced clinicians know, it is possible for clinical work to retrigger a post-traumatic reaction. Such an experience during the early or middle time frame of client psychoeducation about BPD would be therapeutically counterproductive. The emotional demands on the client who integrates a still traumatic experience are considerable. Self-management therapy usually waits to deal with this aspect of BPD until the later stages of therapy. In this vein it is important for the clinician to assess whether anxiety, fear, shame, or other negative emotions are part of a larger PTSD condition or whether these emotions can be separated from PTSD.

PSYCHOEDUCATION AND LIFESTYLE CHANGES VERSUS PSYCHIC REBUILDING

BPD is not a disorder that is cured. Rather, it is managed through lifestyle stability, knowledge about BPD, improved self skills, and occasionally, psychiatric medication. There is some belief among clinicians that aging into the forties and fifties ameliorates BPD characteristics. It seems more likely that such an "aging solution" is an artifact of a stable lifestyle.

Psychoeducation about BPD characteristics is a central and ongoing part of self-management therapy. Because of splitting, memory gaps, perceptual distortions, and emotionally extreme reactions, the need to repeat psychoeducation information is an ongoing process for borderline clients. It is this clinician's experience that splitting blocks awareness and response generalization in borderline clients while encouraging stimulus generalization, although the latter generalization is usually poorly related to reality.

Self-management therapy is more a therapy of teaching and doing, while psychoanalytic-influenced therapy is more a therapy of interpretation and insight. While the latter sees stress as a force necessary for psychic change, self-management therapy recognizes the disproportionate negative impact of stress on borderline clients (Goldstein, 1985, p. 194). Homework between therapy sessions is the major medium of therapeutic action. A major self skills deficit of many borderline clients is limited self-initiation and follow-through. As a consequence, many borderline clients get caught in dead-end or abusive relationships, jobs, or roles. Self-management therapy is designed to provide psychological and strategic support for making successful lifestyle changes.

It is unclear to this writer why so many clients with BPD are so resistant to self-directed change. Given the low threshold for boredom that is a frequent characteristic of BPD, many of these clients appear for psychotherapy trapped in a Catch-22 vise. They are afraid to initiate desired-for changes in their lives, even as they lack the interest to live their current lives with committed energy.

Psychoanalytic-influenced therapy with borderline clients continues to pursue the largely unproductive goal of psychic rebirth or psychic reparenting. After nearly 6 decades of trying to reach this therapeutic goal with borderline clients, the limited success seems simply to have turned many therapists against working with borderline clients. Self-management therapy addresses this near community-wide "blaming the victim" bias among mental health clinicians by establishing reliably reachable goals.

CLOSED END THERAPY VERSUS OPEN END THERAPY

As noted in the previous section, borderline clients have enormous difficulty with follow-through, continuity, and commitment. These self and behavioral limitations must be kept in mind when planning and conducting therapy. A major difference between psychoanalytic-influenced therapy and self-management therapy is that the former is much more open-ended while the latter is much more time limited. Concerning psychoanalytic-influenced therapy with borderline clients, Kreisman and Straus note that "treatment sessions are stormy, frustrating and unpredictable ... most psychotherapists agree that effective treatment requires at least several years" (1989, p. 119).

This quote does not apply to self-management therapy. With its more focused approach, therapy can be packaged into "projects" or around specific BPD characteristics. This "packaging" or boundary setting component allows for therapy breaks, flexible scheduling of appointments, and titrating the emotional intensity of sessions. While borderline clients are not given specific time parameters for length of therapy, any therapy on a weekly basis that lasts longer than 18–24 months suggests one of two things—either the therapy is not effective or there is a dual diagnosis condition that requires different therapeutic energy. The psychotherapists that Kreisman and Straus are referring to in the preceding paragraph would be psychoanalytically influenced. Perhaps the myth about BPD that will be the hardest to negate is the belief among clinicians that working with borderline clients is stormy, frustrating, and unpredictable. Convincing communities of mental health professionals that stormy therapy with borderline clients is an iatrogenic factor of the type of therapy being conducted will not be easy. In essence, our clinical knowledge about borderline client reactions to psychotherapy is, in fact, the reaction of these clients to psychoanalytic-influenced psychotherapy.

Psychoanalytic-influenced therapy makes much of a rather definitive therapy termination process. In self-management therapy the end of therapy as the client has become adjusted is clear. However, this end is presented more as a break than as a termination. "I'm here. Call me if I can help," sets a clear boundary while avoiding a then or later abandonment experience.

INITIAL THERAPY ON RELATIONSHIPS; LATER THERAPY ON SELF ISSUES

Psychoanalytic-influenced therapy is a therapy of intrapsychic change. In its purest form it would interpret as resistance a borderline client's desire to focus therapy on helping to solve a lifestyle problem (Kernberg, 1967, pp. 679–681). Self-management therapy recognizes BPD as a self disorder. However, the sequencing of this therapy is from personal experiences and lifestyle issues while only later addressing specific self disorder issues. Self issues are handled in self-management therapy through a combination of cognitive techniques, structured homework experiences, and in vivo experiences that are discussed and possibly reframed within therapy. However, the focus of therapy for any one borderline client can, in fact, show wide variation from one client to the next. As Goldstein noted, psychoanalysis is designed for neurotic clients, not borderline clients (1985, p. 196). Though self-management therapy has a definite structure, its application lacks the rigidity so often associated with traditional psychoanalysis. In fact, the therapy boundary issues that seem to beleaguer so many therapist-borderline client relationships usually reflect the therapist's failure to address, in a timely manner, boundary setting/boundary maintenance concerns.

Self-management therapy begins with a focus on one of the BPD diagnostic characteristics. If the client presents in crisis, or if a crisis occurs very soon after beginning therapy, the substantive focus of the therapy is on managing the crisis. External (e.g., job problems, financial difficulties, addictive behaviors, etc.) issues or relationship issues are addressed first in self-management therapy. With either focus the emotional intensity of the early phases of therapy can be modulated more easily. The path of therapy is to move toward working with the deficits in the various self functions and to help clients see the connection between these deficits and their problems in daily living.

INTERACTIONAL AND HOMEWORK-BASED THERAPY VERSUS INTERPRETATIONAL AND INSIGHT THERAPY

There are two ways the emotional intensity of self-management therapy is titrated. One way is to keep a client–environment focus and the other way is to make liberal use of homework between sessions. Since the therapeutic relationship is not considered a healing force in self-management therapy, it is not given a lot of therapy time. Perhaps the issue that would dictate more therapeutic time being devoted to the therapy relationship would be excessive client dependency on or idealization of the therapist by the borderline client. Failure by the therapist to defuse these interpersonal issues inevitably leads to therapy threatening encounters later.

Interpretation is to psychoanalytic-influenced therapy as discussing the meaning of a client experience or challenging an action-oriented change is to self-management therapy. Interpretation plays a minor role in self-management therapy. On the other hand, explanation plays a major role. Explanation is used to psychoeducate clients about BPD and to document instances of borderline behavior. It has been this clinician's experience that clients with BPD either blame themselves excessively for their problems in living or they project the fault for their problems onto other people or environmental circumstances. A goal of explanation is to help clients develop an integrated person-environment understanding of their problems.

Clients' failure to do homework always is considered a manifestation of their BPD, even though there are instances when clients have sound reasons for not following through. At issue in such instances is client willingness to have his or her life governed by crises or lesser self-interests at the expense of therapy-based self-interest. Handling homework non-compliance must be done forthrightly but gently so as not to generate an iatrogenic shame experience. The explanation clients give for not following through with homework usually reveals the role that splitting, projection, passivity, and denial/avoidance play in the client's coping style. These psychological coping techniques seem to play a central role in the psychological style of many borderline clients.

RECOGNIZING AND LABELING SHAME VERSUS GENERATING AND DECREASING AGGRESSION

As noted previously, the traditional concept of BPD has identified unmetabolized aggression as its core emotion (Kernberg, 1967). Self-management therapy conceptualizes and treats shame as the core emotion in BPD. Anger and rage are recognized as prevalent emotions but they are seen as self-projective defensive strategies against the more debilitating emotion of shame. If the aggression or rage or anger is worked through therapeutically without attending to the underlying shame, all that the therapy has done is to make borderline clients more susceptible to shame experiences. It is shame, not "excessive oral aggression," that is the biggest threat to the premature end or disruption of therapy.

Because of the nature of shame (e.g., collapse of structures of the self, identity change, denial, etc.) its identification, labeling, and management within therapy is simultaneously delicate and difficult. A client's realization of shame can be the source of severe secondary shame. Also making shame discovery work difficult is the variation in sensations, expressions, and experiences that characterize shame. In therapy the cognitive challenge frequently is to convince clients to relabel experiences as shame that have been labeled more safely in other ways. The behavioral challenge is to get borderline clients to experiment with new behaviors. The self-challenge is to improve self-efficacy, which refers to developing clients' expectations that certain behaviors will help them in reaching their goals and that they themselves will be effective in doing such behaviors.

Shame and narcissism interpenetrate the experiences of the individual to generate both self-identity and self-esteem. The psychoanalytic concept of shame is that this emotion is primitive and active during the early infancy period. Developmentally, guilt soon predominates and relegates shame to the backwaters of psychological development. Psychoanalysts consider shame largely irrelevant to the occurrence of psychopathology, focusing instead on the role of guilt and aggression in psychiatric disorders.

Self-management therapy considers shame a formative psychological force. While healthy shame helps place realistic limitations on individuals, their behaviors, and their lifestyles, toxic shame splits, tears, or blocks the development of integrated self and psychological functions. In essence, shame disrupts the continuity of individuality by splitting a person's self into some condition of inadequacy, irrelevance, insignificance, impotence, or ineptness while simultaneously generating a defensive response to this deficiency state. A pattern of shame defense responses can produce a false self. The false selves of borderline clients are concerned with image management, not with the expression of individuals' authentic wants and preferences. Self-management therapy is concerned with identifying borderline clients' false selves and integrating these functions with the clients' real self functions.

FOSTER INDEPENDENCE AND EMPOWERMENT VERSUS PASSIVITY AND DEPENDENCE

Two major self deficits in borderline clients are self-determination and self-competence. The entire premise underlying self-management therapy is that all borderline clients can improve these two sets of self skills. In fact, enhancing client independence and power is the major therapeutic rationale for neutralizing transferential forces in self-management therapy.

The free association technique in psychoanalytic-infused therapy promotes client passivity and dependence. In this sense this form of therapy functions more as a cocoon for borderline clients while self-management therapy serves more as a springboard. In fact, in the latter type of therapy, client passivity in therapy is addressed specifically with assertiveness training.

Psychoanalytic-influenced therapy, through iatrogenic regression, further reduces the self-determination and self-competence of borderline clients. Given the psychoanalytic assumption that the developmental damage that caused BPD occurred very early in childhood, borderline clients, through therapy techniques and symbolism, are to integrate their split opposites. Presumably, this integration occurs by interpretation-based insight.

On the other hand, self-management therapy is action-oriented. The primary manner of changing is assumed to be through action-generated insight. It is for this reason that homework plays such a central role in this type of therapy. Because of the prevalence of psychological splitting, many clients with BPD gyrate between passivity and impulsivity in initiating and sustaining behavior. Among its several objectives, self-management therapy seeks to modulate the daily behavior of such clients.

In conclusion, some comments are in order on the most significant countertransferential subject facing therapists who work with borderline clients—that of client telephone calls to the therapist between sessions. For all the boundary-setting skills trained clinicians have, it is perplexing to this clinician why so many of us have so much difficulty successfully setting and maintaining limits around telephone contact with borderline clients. The generally held belief that borderline clients need to have voice or visual contact between sessions because of a lack of "object constancy" (an inability to evoke an emotionally satisfying image of the physically absent therapist) has not provided an adequate explanation for this clinician. At any one time I have 15–20 outpatient borderline clients in my caseload. I seldom receive phone calls from these clients. The few phone calls that I do receive are invariably around some lifestyle crisis, usually involving a major abandonment danger, or because of the presence of overwhelming emotions such as depression, anxiety, or fear.

The subject of client telephone calls will be discussed in more detail in Chapter 8. This issue of invasive telephone calls to therapists by borderline clients can be the consequence of two conditions. First, the calls reflect the therapist's failure to provide borderline clients with sufficient emotional safety and relationship structure to function in the short term. Second, the need for telephone contact may be an iatrogenic feature of therapy sessions where the emotional intensity level is set too intensely by the therapist. While therapists may be able to contain their emotions at the end of a session and contain them until the next session, the borderline client may be less able to do so. In this sense, then, telephone calls simply may be clients' efforts to get closure or to develop emotional containment around issues discussed in therapy sessions.

REFERENCES

Bandura, A. (1977). Self-efficacy: Towards a unifying theory of behavioral change. *Psychological Review, 84*(2), 193–215.

Chatham, P. M. (1989). *Treatment of the borderline personality.* Northvale, NJ: Jason Aronson.

Dyregrov, A., & Mitchell, J. T. (1992). Work with traumatized children—psychological effects and coping strategies. *Journal of Traumatic Stress, 5*(1), 5–17.

Goldstein, E. G. (1990). *Borderline disorders: Clinical models and techniques.* New York: The Guilford Press.

Goldstein, W. N. (1985). *An introduction to the borderline conditions.* Northvale, NJ: Jason Aronson.

Gunderson, J. G. (1984). *Borderline personality disorder.* Washington, DC: American Psychiatric Press.

Kernberg, O. (1967). Borderline personality organization. *Journal of the American Psychoanalytic Association, 15,* 641–685.

Kreisman, J. J., & Straus, H. (1989). *I hate you—don't leave me.* Los Angeles: Price Stern Sloan.

Mahler, M. S. (1971). A study of the separation-individuation process. *The Psychoanalytic Study of the Child, 26,* 405.

Terr, L. C. (1989). Treating psychic trauma in children: A preliminary discussion. *Journal of Traumatic Stress, 2*(1), 3–20.

Volkan, V. D. (1987). *Six steps in the treatment of borderline personality organization.* Northvale, NJ: Jason Aronson.

Yule, W., & Williams, R. M. (1990). Post-traumatic stress reactions in children. *Journal of Traumatic Stress, 3*(2), 279–295.

Therapy Goals for Borderline Personality Disorder

6

P rognosis in psychotherapy pertains to the markers used to measure outcome or progress. Waldinger and Gunderson (1984, p. 190) noted that "only three studies of a small number of borderline patients who completed intensive (2–5 times a week) psychotherapy" had been published.

Prognosis for borderline clients has been shaped largely by the experiences of psychoanalytic therapists. Based upon his work with the Menninger Foundation study of Psychotherapy Research Project, Kernberg identified five elements pertinent to making a prognosis for the outcome of psychotherapy for borderline clients:

1. descriptive characterological diagnosis
2. degree and quality of ego weakness
3. degree and quality of superego pathology
4. quality of object relationships and
5. skill and personality of the therapist. (1971, p. 595)

The focus on client psychogenic factors (1–4) and therapy iatrogenic factors (5) are obvious. A very glaring omission is the relative absence of client life circumstances as forces effecting the outcome of therapy. The following quote by Woollcott, written 14 years after Kernberg's comments but quoting the very same study used by Kernberg, noted:

The importance of the patient's life circumstances during treatment has generally been underestimated as a prognostic factor, but especially in borderline cases and other more seriously disturbed patients. The psychotherapy research project of the Menninger Foundation noted life circumstances during the therapy as a significant prognostic factor, strongly affecting treatment outcome. Absence of significant supportive relationships, or highly disturbed or destructive ones present severe obstacles for psychotherapy. (Woollcott, 1985, p.19)

Woollcott noted also that a childhood history of abusive trauma for clients with BPD, especially by parents, was particularly prognostic of a negative therapy outcome (1985, pp. 23–24).

It seems likely that life circumstances that affect therapy are not limited to the types of relationships borderline clients are in during therapy. Being appropriately employed, having work successes, an adequate income and having adequate mental health insurance benefits to help pay the cost of therapy and to insure the continuation of therapy also would seem to be significant prognostic indicators that affect therapy outcome. Participation in community organizations, the passionate pursuit of a hobby or special interest, and freedom from obsessive or compulsive practices, including all types of addictions, also would seem to have some prognostic value in determining the outcome of therapy for borderline clients. Not experiencing the loss of a loved one or not experiencing a traumatic event during the course of therapy are also likely to impact the continuation and progress of therapy.

In their 1984 article, Waldinger and Gunderson (p. 192) analyzed data provided by 11 therapists who had 78 borderline (both BPD and Kernberg's borderline personality organization) clients that successfully completed intensive psychotherapy. The therapists assessed their clients on ego functioning, behavior, object relations, and sense of self. In total, the therapists treated 790 borderline clients. Over half stayed in intensive psychotherapy (more than one session a week) for over 6 months.

Of the 78 borderline clients, each, on average, was in therapy 4 ½ years with sessions three times a week. This sample of 78 clients averaged more than 700 individual sessions per client. Despite this tremendous investment of therapy resources, Waldinger and Gunderson note:

> While a majority of patients terminated treatment gradually (56%) rather than precipitously (44%), more patients in this sample terminated treatment against their therapist's advice (60%) than with the therapist's approval (40%). (1984, p. 193)

These authors asked both the 11 therapists and the 78 clients why therapy ended. Clients' reasons are given followed by therapists' reasons:

> The most common reason given by patients (51%) for termination was that they had improved and were satisfied with the results of therapy. Another 27 percent left treatment ostensibly due to life changes which were unrelated to treatment (e.g. moves or job changes). Nine percent said they terminated because of family opposition to treatment.
>
> Therapists likewise judged that in 50 percent of cases, treatment ended because the patient had improved and the therapist was satisfied with the results. Therapists believed that a therapeutic impasse was responsible for the termination of therapy in 22 percent of cases. They reported 18 percent of patients to have terminated because of reasons unrelated to treatment (e.g., moves or job changes) and they felt that in 5 percent of cases, termination could be attributed to family opposition. (Waldinger & Gunderson, 1984, p. 193)

Despite the above quote and figures the authors make the following *non sequitur* comments about the sample of 78 clients:

> Moreover, none of the patients was rated as having achieved an optimal state of health at the close of treatment. And even in these 'successful' cases, most patients were judged to have terminated prematurely . . . Even in the hands of experts, the patient who gets much better is the exception rather than the rule. (Waldinger & Gunderson, 1984, p. 197)

While the above series of quotes concerning the 78 borderline clients who completed psychotherapy seemed balanced, Waldinger (1987, p. 268), in an article 3 years later, made the following comment about this sample: "Borderline patients are notoriously difficult to engage in psychotherapy, and they commonly flee treatment shortly after it has begun."

This quote simply is not supported by the research data. Not to be overlooked in Waldinger and Gunderson's larger sample of 790 borderline clients is the fact that over 50% (perhaps 400) stayed in therapy for over 6 months, with presumably three sessions per week. This cohort of approximately 400 borderline clients averaged 80–85 psychotherapy sessions before terminating. Referring back to the "successful" subsample of 78, it is not clear that there is a positive relationship between borderline clients' improvement in therapy and therapists' judgment of when to terminate therapy. Certainly, if the goal is some "optimal level of mental health functioning," it is conceivable that no client with BPD would ever reach this standard for terminating therapy.

It appears to this clinician that Waldinger and Gunderson's data speak more to the expectations psychotherapists have toward borderline clients and to the demands of psychoanalytic-influenced therapy than to the willingness of borderline clients to complete such therapy. Note that the comparison standard used by Waldinger and Gunderson was not another psychiatric diagnostic group. Rather, the comparison standard for "successfully completing therapy" seemed to be the non-quantified expectations of the therapists. The fact that over one-half of the clinical population of 780 borderline clients average 80–85 individual psychotherapy sessions seems to have been ignored by the authors. The cognitive, behavioral, and existential psychotherapists with whom I am familiar would not label their clients "premature terminators" if they stopped therapy after 80–85 sessions. The open-ended nature of psychoanalytic-infused therapy may make it difficult for clients to terminate their own therapy without it appearing to be premature. Nonetheless, the image is imprinted deeply in the sociogenic consciousness of therapists' professional communities that borderline clients terminate before they should. The presumption seems clear in the Waldinger and Gunderson article that therapists control the therapy termination decision for borderline clients.

It seems that, data notwithstanding, the psychoanalytic-inspired belief that borderline clients leave therapy prematurely or disruptively has a real hold on the psyche of mental health clinicians. The conclusion that borderline clients are difficult to engage in therapy still was reached, despite an average of 4½ years in psychotherapy with more than 700 sessions per client in a form of therapy contraindicated for borderline clients.

This writer's review of the psychotherapy literature revealed minimal attention toward measurable criteria for successful therapy with borderline clients. If Waldinger's standard—"an optimal state of health or functioning"—is the implicit standard in the field, perhaps the problem of having successful therapy is with the standard and not with this class of clients.

The influence of psychoanalytic theory and beliefs on setting therapy goals for treating BPD has created a split between the daily lives of borderline clients and their therapy. The major focus of psychoanalytic-influenced therapy with BPD is intrapsychic. Such therapy intends to complete the development of object relations, to make the self more autonomous or resilient or to improve various ego functions relative to the experience of emotions and the processing and use of information in decision-making. Much less emphasis is placed on behavioral and lifestyle variables. In their research Waldinger and Gunderson used as a measure of work effectiveness a variable ranging from "productive in vocational roles" to "impulsive disruption of . . . vocational roles under stress" to "poor work history" (1984, p. 202).

However, it is important to point out that it is unlikely that the psychoanalytic therapy provided their sample actually focused on work-related issues. Teaching borderline clients anger management, impulse control, disruption of their idealization/devaluation cycles and recognition of their abandonment concerns relative to work peers and managers simply is not a part of psychoanalytic therapy. Concerning guidelines for measuring successful therapy, psychoanalytic-influenced therapy does not take a practical problem-solving approach. Instead, the therapy focus is on identifying the autobiographical basis for current behaviors with special interest on parent/child experiences and how these experiences may be being repeated in the client's adult life. It is usually left to clients to apply their therapy-founded, self-knowledge to their current life. In fact, traditional psychoanalysis considers a focus on the client's current life as a form of resistance.

There is a serious psychological flaw in using psychoanalytic theory to set therapy goals for borderline clients. The major therapeutic focus on such therapy will be on clients' intrapsychic—object relations, ego, and self—development. The presumption is that with such development appropriate behavior and lifestyle responses will occur. However, with the legacy of splitting that is such an integral part of BPD, it is not reasonable to expect response generalization by borderline clients from their therapy to their lives outside of therapy without specific therapeutic support and coaching. For example, defensive splitting is caused by circumstances other than the absence of object constancy. Defensive splitting occurs with people who are under contemporary threats to their self-identify and self-esteem. Defensive splitting also occurs with people who are experiencing excessive anxiety, anger, shame, depression, fear, or other stressful emotions. As a consequence, for therapy to be maximally effective with borderline clients, it should minimize the opportunities for splitting.

With borderline clients, a therapy that integrates therapy goals with clients' immediate life circumstances promises the least disruptive and most successful therapy experience. Such a therapy model reduces the diluting impact of splitting. Shame attacks, abandonment panic and rage episodes—such a familiar part of psychoanalytic-influenced therapy with borderline clients—are mitigated greatly by keeping therapy both pragmatic and problem-solving for borderline clients. Providing a pragmatic and problem-solving focus in therapy does not negate an important role for insight and understanding of childhood influences on current behavior and lifestyle circumstances. The objective in self-management therapy, however, is to keep the therapy focused on the contemporary.

A more difficult therapeutic concern is what constitutes an appropriate standard of care in determining when a borderline client has had enough therapy or when the therapy is successful. With the limitations developing in the 1990s around the accessibility to mental health services, weekly therapy for 4½ years (as was available to the sample in the Waldinger and Gunderson study) will be available to fewer and fewer borderline clients. Rather than having an explicit or an implicit standard of "optimum mental health" as a therapy goal, perhaps goals that meet a "good enough" standard will be sufficient to allow borderline clients to live autonomous and self-determining lives. Self-efficacy that is "good enough" will support such lifestyles for borderline clients.

If autonomy and self-determination in living are goals of therapy for borderline clients, then the therapy process and content must extend into clients' daily lives. Whether at the psychological level or at the lifestyle level, the presence of splitting in borderline clients works against integrated functioning or integrated living. As noted, psychoanalytic-influenced psychotherapy with borderline clients has primarily an intrapsychic focus. It would stand to reason that the effectiveness of this type of therapy would be measured by specific ego, self, or object relations functions. Clearly, there are people who have these functions adequately developed who are not living satisfying lives.

In the largest study yet published on BPD, Stone (1990, p. 1) traced the follow-up adjustment of 500 "consecutively admitted patients hospitalized during the years 1963 to 1976 . . . at the New York State Psychiatric Institute." Of this number 298 were diagnosed as borderline. The patients in this study were exposed to psychoanalytic therapy three times a week. Yet, in evaluating the effectiveness of this therapy, Stone, in part, looked at these patients' subsequent work histories, marital histories, and whether or not they became parents. It is highly unlikely that traditional psychoanalytic therapy, especially in an inpatient setting, focused on these lifestyle variables. To expect response generalization from improved ego, self, and object relations functions to improved functioning in current life circumstances of the borderline client, is to ignore the realities of BPD. The impact of splitting, the level of environmental stress, the inadequacy of stress management skills, the extent of relationship and social support, the extent to which clients' post-traumatic stress disorder has been treated, are just a few variables affecting post-therapy adjustment. To measure the effectiveness of psychoanalysis or psychoanalytic therapy by looking at work, marital, and fertility data is tantamount to measuring the height of individuals by having them step on scales. The measures of outcome are related minimally to the processes that make up psychoanalytic therapy. Psychoanalytic therapy probably is evaluated best by using measures of object relations rather than measures of lifestyle adjustment.

Self-management therapy is intended to integrate borderline clients' world of therapy with their daily lives. The standards used to assess the effectiveness of self-management therapy are "good enough" functioning by borderline clients in the major areas of their lives. The "good enough" standard is very similar to the concept of the same name put forth by the psychoanalyst David Winnicott (1965) in the 1950s and 1960s.

In self-management therapy the "good enough" standard is intended to be in the middle range of a dimension anchored at the top end by the terms "optimal," "perfect," or "ideal" and at the lower end by the terms "inadequate," "ineffective," or "harmful." The "good enough" standard is intended to give therapists an anchor to assess therapy outcome that may be shielded from the idealization/devaluation phase so characteristic of BPD and that is such a potentially disruptive iatrogenic force in therapy with borderline clients. This same standard of "good enough" provides clients with a non-shaming alternative to the splitting induced idealization/devaluation cycle that bedevils so many borderline clients in their therapy experiences.

Every outpatient borderline client with whom I have worked therapeutically or diagnostically has had at least one major area of their lives functioning at a "good enough" level. A major objective of self-management therapy is to bring this fact of "good enough" functioning through the web of BPD distortions and to the full attention of the client. Then, by psychoeducating clients about their BPD, identifying any existing post-traumatic stress disorder, and helping clients to change or to self-manage their psychological or lifestyle activities that do not meet a "good enough" standard, clients' therapy and daily lives become more integrated while also improving in quality.

Specific therapy goals, of course, will differ for various clients in self-management therapy. However, the one overarching goal for all borderline clients is a "good enough" understanding of BPD and a growing ability to recognize and to manage the borderline influences in their therapy and daily lives. The borderline influences are those described in current diagnostic manuals.

Many clients with BPD also have a dual diagnosis. Most frequently the dual diagnosis may include an affective disorder such as anxiety, depression, panic, social phobia, substance abuse of alcohol, prescription or illegal drugs, or another personality disorder. For self-management purposes it is important that clients learn how their dual diagnoses interact with each other.

There are other "good enough" standards that can be applied to assess the effectiveness of self-management therapy. Some examples of such standards include: clients' "good enough" self-management of their thoughts, feelings, and behaviors; "good enough" participation in the work role, citizen volunteer role, church role or other chosen adult role; "good enough" participation in non-abusive relationships; "good enough" functioning as a parent; clients' "good enough" acceptance of abusive experiences in their backgrounds.

An important therapy goal for the clinician is to help clients avoid developing an incapacitating dependency on the clinician. The responsibility of the clinician to titrate successfully the client's therapeutic dependency is important. In traditional therapy with borderline clients, the clinician was to facilitate client dependency via encouraging a passive and regressive therapy role. Self-management therapy considers these iatrogenic forces harmful in two ways for clients with BPD. First, the regressive experiences can generate therapy-induced shame, which often manifests in anger or rage expressions (the infamous borderline explosion). Second, the passivity undermines the development of client self-efficacy. It is a form of therapy-induced splitting to impose passivity expectations on borderline clients in their therapy while expecting them to develop outside of therapy, assertive behavior intended to foster self-efficacy.

The issue of borderline clients prematurely disrupting or terminating their own therapy must be addressed. The clinical folk wisdom that calls on borderline clients' psychogenic factors to explain why such clients won't stay in therapy ignores an obvious paradox: Why would a client with BPD risk an abandonment experience with a therapist by unilaterally stopping therapy? It is the contention of this clinician that iatrogenically produced shame factors are probably the major factors that prematurely end borderline clients' therapy, not client psychogenic factors. As noted in Chapter 3, it is possible for shame to be psychogenically, as well as interpersonally, activated. It is far more reasonable in a therapy setting for clients with BPD to have their shame activated by iatrogenic therapy factors. Clinician-induced shame attacks occur easily in borderline clients if the clinician perceives such clients as having an excess of hostility or aggression, a developmental deficit, or a developmental conflict.

Psychoanalytic conceptions of BPD do not recognize shame as a major psychological factor in BPD. Consequently, shame dynamics are not considered by most clinicians as being an integral reason for therapy being disrupted or terminated. Because the historical roots of psychoanalysis were planted in the soil of aggression and guilt, shame has become the neglected emotion of mental health treatment. As noted in Chapter 3, the close association between narcissism, shame, and self-development should provide an easy conceptual bridge for seeing shame in a central role in BPD. A second issue around therapy termination is, "Who has major responsibility for determining when therapy stops?" With psychoanalytic-influenced therapy, the responsibility seems clearly to rest with the therapist. Clients with BPD are considered to have an infantile pre-oedipal disorder. From this conception of the disorder, the paternalistic assumptions by therapists trained in psychoanalytic traditions of who terminates therapy is but a short step.

Self-management therapy considers the therapy termination decision to be mutual, with the client taking the lead. In self-management therapy, termination is not an abrupt process, but rather is handled more as a maintenance phase of therapy. In the maintenance phase clients initiate therapy sessions on an "as needed" basis.

To determine what is "good enough" for a particular client requires the participation of both therapist and client. On the therapist's side are pressures associated with the client's BPD diagnosis that may lead to therapy goals that lack a "good enough" standard. For example, trying to keep a borderline client in therapy—helping/hoping a client does not have a rage attack toward the therapist—is a therapy goal that lacks a "good enough" standard.

On the client side are pressures pushing for perfectionism or pressures pushing for "getting by" standards. The challenge is to set therapy goals with a standard of "good enough" that is mid-range on the perfection/inadequate dimension.

With self-management therapy one of the ways the continuity of therapy is managed is by providing for "therapy vacations." As self-management therapy goals tend to be concrete, reaching a goal is identified more easily than in psychoanalytic-influenced therapy. With any borderline client, therapy goals usually number more than one. As a consequence therapy can be "packaged" into subunits and broken up in time. In fact, a major act of client empowerment is for the therapist to show confidence in clients by agreeing to a break from therapy. Such a break is presented as temporary with the client having access to the therapist on an "as needed" basis.

For self-management therapy the "good enough" standard as a therapy goal is a combination of subjective and objective measures. Clients' reported experiences, outside of therapy, verified by a third party when and if possible, are one objective measure of "good enough" progress in therapy. Who determines what is "good enough" touches one of the power dimensions in the therapist-client relationship. Probably the most consistent and most often addressed subject in the clinical literature on BPD is the regularity with which clients prematurely terminate therapy. The previously quoted research by Waldinger and Gunderson addressed the issue of who determines when there has been enough therapy. In the sample of 78 clients with BPD or borderline personality organization the authors report, " . . . a majority of patients terminated treatment gradually (56%) rather than precipitously (44%), more patients in this sample terminated against their therapist's advice (60%) than with the therapist's approval" (Waldinger & Gunderson, 1984, p. 193). These figures raise the iatrogenic question of why the therapist might be a better judge than the client as to when there has been enough therapy. Perhaps the issue of borderline clients leaving therapy prematurely should be reframed to say "clients leaving therapy before the therapist is ready for them to leave." Perhaps the concern in the professional literature around borderline clients leaving therapy prematurely is really a concern about therapists retaining the power to terminate therapy. After all, the decision to end therapy has significant economic consequences for both therapist and client and significant lifestyle implications for the client.

The idea that therapists know better than their borderline clients when therapy should end is an interesting one. Perhaps it arises from the conception of borderline being an infantile disorder with primitive psychological coping mechanisms. From this conception it is a short step to the belief that the therapist knows borderline clients' best interests better than clients know their own.

REFERENCES

Kernberg, O. F. (1971). Prognostic considerations regarding borderline personality organization. *Journal of American Psychoanalytic Association, 19*(4), 595–635.

Stone, M. H. (1990). *The fate of borderline patients.* New York: The Guilford Press.

Waldinger, J. R. (1987). Intensive psychodynamic therapy with borderline patients: An overview. *American Journal of Psychiatry, 144*(3), 267–274.

Waldinger, R. J., & Gunderson, J. G. (1984). Completed psychotherapies with borderline patients. *American Journal of Psychotherapy, XXXVIII*(2), 190–202.

Winnicott, D. W. (1965). *The maturational processes and the facilitating environment.* New York: International Universities Press.

Woollcott, P., Jr. (1985). Prognostic indicators in the psychotherapy of borderline patients. *American Journal of Psychotherapy, XXXIX*(1), 17–29.

Conducting Therapy with Borderline Personality Disorder Clients

7

The purpose of this chapter is to provide clinicians with a practical framework for working with borderline clients through all phases of the therapy experience. The central contention is that iatrogenic therapy factors and not psychogenic client factors, account for BPD individuals being difficult psychotherapy clients. This chapter describes a therapeutic structure that has purged most psychoanalytic-influenced practices in the face-to-face therapeutic interactions with borderline clients. The immediate consequences for clinician and client are the elimination of acting out, rage episodes, and the elimination of a stultifying level of iatrogenically induced shame/dependency for the client.

"Therapeutic structure" is probably the key feature of the self-management model. Table 7.1 lists the various phases of self-management therapy and the criteria for determining a particular phase of therapy. Although the table gives the appearance of discrete phases, reality is not always that neat and clean. These phases can either overlap, as often happens with diagnosis and treatment, or they can reoccur, as often happens with the diagnosis phase. For example, the self-management model of BPD recognizes that PTSD is a co-occurring dual diagnosis. However, this diagnosis is not made until later in therapy, when the client with BPD has acquired improved coping skills.

TABLE 7.1 Phases of Self-Management Psychotherapy

Phase	Criterion
Pre-Diagnosis	From appointment setting to clinician sharing diagnosis with client
Diagnosis	From communicating diagnosis to client to client acknowledging diagnosis to clinician; note if PTSD may be present
Treatment	All activities promulgated by clinician to address particular BPD characteristics or those of a dual diagnosis; specifically identify PTSD condition and begin its treatment via psychoeducation
Self-Management	All activities engaged in outside therapy sessions by clients that focus on managing specific BPD characteristics or those of a dual diagnosis; would include homework as well as self-initiated actions.
Maintenance	Non-regular therapy contact by client to review or further develop coping skills relative to BPD characteristics or those of a dual diagnosis

It is important to notice in Table 7.1 that the diagnosis phase has two crucial associated components. One is the clinician's documented knowledge of the client's diagnosis and the other is the client's acceptance of this diagnosis. Both conditions must be met before the diagnostic phase is completed.

GUIDELINES FOR STRUCTURING SELF-MANAGEMENT THERAPY

The following guidelines assist clinicians in replacing psychoanalytic influences with therapeutic influences more compatible with BPD.

BPD is an Adult Self Disorder with no Assumption of a Pre-Oedipal or Infancy Disability

There are no scientifically verified theories of what causes BPD. It seems likely most clinicians have developed their own theory based upon their personal clinical experience. Clinician attitude may be largely non-verbal and may be an important medium through which to communicate shame in an unintentional way. If clinicians view clients with BPD as having a developmental disorder of early childhood, it seems virtually impossible for clinicians not to expect, at least, instances of childlike behavior from their clients.

Considering BPD to be an adult self disorder should enhance clinician attitudes of equality and acceptance toward such clients. It is very likely that with the forces of projection and projective identification operating between clinician and client, clinician attitude could be one of several triggers that sets off the "borderline rages" that are such a familiar part of traditional therapy with BPD clients.

Clinician Adapts a Proactive Style Throughout Therapy

There is no constructive role for technical neutrality in the clinician's style with BPD clients. As an antidote to excessive anxiety that unstructured interaction can create, clinicians are most effective with BPD clients when providing clear leadership. Long lapses of silence, forcing the client to structure the clinical session and asking clients only introspective questions (e.g., "How does that make you feel?") are all examples of a passive or reactive clinician style. With borderline clients such a style seems to make it difficult for them to feel connected or valued. Anxiety and shame appear to be two client emotions that are generated by passive or reactive clinicians. An example of a proactive clinician would be one who brings up the subject of telephone calls between sessions. If clinicians set guidelines on telephone calls (no telephone calls between sessions is neither a reasonable nor flexible guideline), clients usually will follow them unless the clinical relationship is faulty. A proactive clinician style also models self-efficacious behavior for clients, which increases the compatibility between clinician style and the goal of therapy.

Therapy Sessions Are Tightly Structured

Individuals with BPD seem to respond well to structure that is enabling rather than coercive. There are four types of structure that clinicians can bring to bear in their therapy sessions with BPD clients. The most immediate type is interactional. Clinicians are sufficiently responsive to their clients so that there is true dialogue rather than a more stilted question and answer format or free association monologue by the client. A major purpose of interactional structure is to develop a partnership between clinician and client.

A less immediate type of structure is content. Free association, or its variant of letting the client select the content, usually is not productive in work with BPD clients. The exception for letting clients select the therapy topic is when the client is in a crisis. Typically, the discussion from the previous session, the relevant BPD diagnostic features, and assigned homework will shape the content of a specific session.

In fact, homework is an important source of therapy structure. The issue with homework should never deteriorate to a compliance versus noncompliance issue. Rather, homework is a major medium for developing self-efficacy. Any homework "failure" should be linked to the relevant BPD feature.

A fourth type of structure clinicians should employ with their BPD clients is time. Therapy involves time-limited relationships. Clinicians regularly and almost off handedly should be preparing their clients to terminate therapy. Clinicians often fail to draw the line with BPD clients between feeling safe (which is therapeutically important) and becoming dependent (which is therapeutically shaming). In a therapy relationship that may last 2 years or longer, it is important that clinicians provide regular reality checks to their BPD clients that therapy is not forever.

Maintain a Mild to Moderate Intensity Level in Therapy

The chronic problems of interpersonal boundaries that are so much a part of BPD must be addressed by clinicians. It appears that many clients with BPD lack the ability to modulate their own levels of emotional intensity. It becomes an important therapeutic task of the clinician to set and to maintain a functional level of emotional intensity for their clients. BPD clients have high regressive potential in emotionally charged settings. Prevention and avoidance of such intensity in the therapeutic relationship is crucial if the therapy setting is to teach self-efficacy and to avoid iatrogenically produced disruption. BPD clients will respond non-eventfully to emotionally significant content presented in an emotionally controlled setting. It may be helpful to think of BPD clients as having a limit on the intensity they can manage and most of that intensity should be preserved for therapeutic content, not expended in therapeutic process.

Identify Concrete Goals and Keep Them in Awareness

A major resource that clinicians bring to therapy with BPD clients is focus. A major disability associated with BPD is difficulty in setting or sustaining focus. Articulating concrete goals is a significant part of interactional structure. Such goals also provide both focus and continuity for clients. Even though therapy may appear to get sidetracked or derailed by a crisis in the client's life, if therapy goals have been developed thoughtfully, crisis intervention is usually very compatible with the client's and clinician's goals for self-management therapy. Because of the impact of splitting, avoidance, and denial on the personality style of BPD clients, frequent reminders of therapy goals are necessary. It is important, also, that the standard of "good enough," detailed in Chapter 6, be expressed and embraced by clinicians. The "either-or" personality style of most BPD clients tends to make them "closet perfectionists" as their pre-therapy ability to accept "good enough" is usually quite limited.

Demonstrate Respectful Humor

Humor can play paradoxical roles in the therapeutic relationship. In self-management therapy humor can serve to dilute the intensity of a subject or an encounter or it can be used to establish a functional level of bonding between clinician and client.

Great care must be exercised when using humor in a therapeutic relationship with BPD clients. As noted in Chapter 3, humor is one of the fronts or defenses employed against shame recognition or shame awareness. As a consequence, clinicians must be as aware as possible of what their motives are for using humor and the likely consequences for their clients. Correspondingly, clinicians must be ready to probe clients as to the multiple meanings associated with clients' use of humor. Shame is always the psychological land mine that must be watched for when humor occurs in a clinical relationship. It is important that the personal expression present in most forms of humor not fall victim to excessive clinical circumspection.

Sustain Silence Only When Client Is Processing

With severely borderline clients therapeutic silence can have a very regressive impact. The therapeutic challenge is to balance the client's need for silence and silence as a force that disintegrates self boundaries. Although there is no research data to support my clinical experience, I have noticed that most of my BPD clients often take longer to process an experience or information than I think they should take. Disregarding clinician impatience as a factor here, the apparent additional time may reflect the impact of splitting or the dissolving of splitting by the client. Either way, silence plays an important role at this point in the client's therapeutic experience. Silence produced by clinician passivity is usually anti-therapeutic with BPD clients.

Use Therapy for Crisis Intervention on an "As Needed" Basis

A central feature of the adult disorder of BPD is a tendency toward instability and crisis. A central function of therapy with BPD clients is to assist in resolving the crisis but also to teach clients crisis resolving and crisis avoiding skills. Because of the impact of splitting and denial in the way BPD clients view their world, many truly do not see their role in generating the crisis. Prone to orient passively (and sometimes helplessly) to their environment, BPD clients can be very hard to convince that, with respect to the current crisis, they are not simply passive victims—again. The role of the therapist in solving the crisis is shaped by a combination of ethical considerations and the stage of the client's therapy. Ethical considerations require more direct intervention if there are homicidal or suicidal dangers. If the crisis appears to be a reoccurrence of a pattern, the clinician may be less inclined to provide direct relief and more inclined to point the pattern out to the client. Therapy usually mirrors life and if BPD clients successfully integrate regular "crises" within their therapy, then clearly there are some serious unattended iatrogenic problems operating within the therapy relationship.

Homework Provides Continuity

As Bandura (1971, p. 195) notes, performance accomplishments are probably the best source for learning self-efficacy. This rationale is the most central to why homework plays such a major role in self-management therapy. Homework also is a medium through which BPD clients can learn self-continuity and how to prioritize activities. Many BPD clients have major difficulty with follow-through. The use of homework provides a goal-oriented, concrete task to help them focus. The implied accountability to the clinician can give them the initial impetus to complete what they said they would do. "Why didn't you do your homework?" is never an appropriate question. Rather, the therapeutic concern is what aspects of BPD are blocking the completion of the homework and what can be done to dissolve the blockage and get the homework completed. Clinicians should never draw a line in the sand and insist that particular homework get done or that it get done in a certain way. Homework is always a means to a larger therapeutic end.

Monitor Therapy Relationship—Defuse Excessive Dependency

Perhaps the single irreversible flaw in a therapeutic relationship with a BPD client is excessive dependency. Dependency with this type of client is an ongoing problem. However, there is a point when the level of dependency becomes both irreversible and anti-therapeutic. At that point consultations for the clinician become appropriate and a plan to transition the client to another clinician should be developed.

Excessive dependency between clinician and BPD client is

so toxic because it is the result of (probably unrecognized) shame that has severely diluted the interpersonal boundaries between clinician and client. While such boundaries can be reestablished, it is this clinician's opinion that a therapeutic relationship cannot be reestablished.

Avoiding excessive dependency may be one of the biggest challenges in working with BPD clients. Virtually ignored in the literature is the issue of financial dependence that the clinician may develop on the client. A good therapeutic relationship with a BPD client means a regular and lengthy source of income for the clinician. Keeping the relationship tilted slightly or significantly toward dependency and away from self-efficacy, is an error easy for clinicians to make. In fact, part of the rationale in self-management therapy for minimizing interpretation and maximizing explanation is to reduce the dependency forces operating within the therapeutic relationship.

Therapy Focus Is Not on the Clinical Relationship

Transference is not a therapeutic force with BPD clients. It is for this reason alone that self-management therapy does not make the clinical relationship a therapeutic focus. The tendency of BPD clients to distort reality is worsened by clinical interactions whose meaning is split from these interactions and located in parent–child relationships of some 20 to 50 years earlier. In addition, transference forces appear to be more intense than the self boundaries of many BPD clients can handle.

There is an exception when self-management therapy does focus on the clinical relationship. If the clinical relationship becomes a problem for the client, then the dynamics of the relationship and the perceptions of the participants must be reviewed. Unrecognized shame or anxiety or an undetected PTSD flashback are the most likely culprits affecting the relationship. Such problems are usually able to be remedied if there is not excessive dependency within the relationship or if the relationship is not in the early formative stages. As a visual model self-management therapy is more of a springboard and less of a cocoon.

Therapy Has a Present to Future Focus Rather Than Past to Present

The near-hackneyed phrase "those who do not know history are doomed to repeat it" has some limited applicability in therapy with BPD clients. The core of psychoanalytic-influenced therapies with BPD clients has sought historical childhood causes for adult BPD features. Furthermore, these traditional therapies have sought to equip BPD adults with early childhood skills or resolve early childhood scars.

In a significant break with tradition, self-management therapy takes a present to future therapeutic focus. BPD is not considered to be a developmental, childhood disorder. Rather, the disorder is seen as an adult self disorder in which certain self and interpersonal skills and identity clarity are lacking. The goal in self-management therapy is to prepare BPD clients for effective daily living. Preparing for the future rather than repairing the past is the therapeutic focus.

Frequent Repetition of Therapy Issues

The major influences of splitting, shame, and denial in BPD have significant impact on both short-term and long-term memory. Avoidance is a major coping mechanism used by many BPD clients and it is for this reason that anxiety, panic, and phobias are such frequent dual diagnoses with BPD.

As noted, self-management therapy focuses on the diagnostic characteristics of BPD. Repeating these characteristics as they manifest in numerous ways in the client's life is a major psychoeducation function of this therapy. Encouraging and repeating how to stop the BPD diagnostic characteristics is another important part of self-management therapy. Also getting BPD clients to experiment with new self-efficacious behavior is yet another form of repetition. When the therapy goals are new self definitions and new self-promoting behaviors, the one or two time approach, which characterizes insight-producing therapies are simply inadequate.

Awareness to Prohibition to New Behaviors

Progress in self-management therapy for BPD clients is specified clearly. Progress occurs initially through increased client awareness about BPD and how it manifests in the client's life. As client awareness increases through psychoeducation, the focus of change itself changes. With their new-found awareness about BPD, clients try to change the frequency, severity, and duration of BPD characteristics. For example, clients focus on stopping their impulsivity or in controlling their anger. The third and last focus of change in self-management therapy is on substituting more effective behavior for the BPD diagnostic characteristics. Of course, increased awareness is the initial focus for change with both shame and PTSD issues. This increase in awareness is followed by a reduction in the impact of these two issues in clients' daily lives.

Table 7.2 provides a general chronology of therapy activities clinicians employ with their BPD clients. This table provides only a guideline as each clinician-client relationship may lead to different emphases.

Table 7.3 matches therapy activities or interventions with each of the BPD diagnostic characteristics. Listed under the event column are conditions associated with or preceding BPD. As a clinician it is very important to remember there is no verified theory of BPD. Self-management therapy represents a clinical theory of intervention for BPD but not a theory of causation.

A brief rationale seems in order why the hypothetical case example presented here is a female client. In Swartz, Blazer, George, and Winfield (1990, p. 258) review of the literature on the prevalence of BPD, the sex of the client is the only demographic variable consistently associated with the BPD diagnosis. These authors noted whether the sample of individuals meeting the criteria for a BPD diagnosis came from the community, an outpatient treatment setting, or inpatient treatment setting females predominate over males in this diagnostic category by about 3:1 (Widiger & Frances, 1989). How much this ratio is "real" versus how much of it is shaped by iatrogenic, clinical factors is an unresolved issue.

CASE EXAMPLE OF SELF-MANAGEMENT THERAPY

The following will include excerpts of hypothetical client-clinician sessions in self-management therapy. For didactic

TABLE 7.2 Overview of Activities in Self-Management Therapy For Each Phase of Therapy

Pre-Diagnosis Phase

1. Determine kind of help client wants, learn about client and formulate a tentative diagnosis.
2. If necessary, possible intervention into lifestyle or behavioral crisis may be required immediately.
3. If dual diagnosis is present and includes substance dependence, an addiction intervention may supersede self-management therapy. While both forms of therapy are compatible with each other, the issue is which to do first. Intervention for an addiction should precede self-management therapy.

Diagnosis Phase

4. Aim to establish a diagnosis and communicate it to client in the first session or as soon as possible.
5. Use latest DSM diagnostic characteristics and document diagnosis in client's history and share it with client.
6. Prepare client for, or discuss with client, possible secondary or iatrogenic shame associated with the BPD diagnosis.
7. Assess for childhood or adulthood unresolved trauma (PTSD), but probably not share with client at this time.

Treatment Phase

8. Treatment is focused first on the one or two BPD diagnostic characteristics that are causing the client the most difficulty.
9. As soon as possible, treatment focuses on each one of the applicable BPD diagnostic features.
10. If at any time during therapy psychotropic medication is needed, referral to a psychiatrist occurs.
11. Psychoeducate on splitting and allied personality mechanisms associated with or interacting with BPD.
12. Explain and show both the primary and auxiliary roles of shame possibly associated with a BPD diagnosis.
13. Help clients recognize and label their more pervasive shame and its variants.
14. Use homework (cognitive, behavioral, experiential) to become aware of or to integrate shame experiences into consciousness, identity, and/or memory.

TABLE 7.2 Continued

15. Monitor and regulate emotional intensity of therapeutic relationship to keep it in mild to moderate range of intensity.
16. Therapy focus is seldom on the therapeutic relationship except for role modeling or positive reinforcement purposes. The therapy relationship is not used for interpretational purposes.
17. On a regular basis, ask clients their view of therapy as a way to monitor the influence of splitting and the level of emotional intensity.
18. Use homework assignments as experiments to self-manage BPD characteristics in daily life.
19. As appropriate, psychoeducate on self-functions and their impairment in BPD.
20. Offer homework to strengthen specific self-functions along with encouraging an assertive style by clients toward clinicians.
21. Use homework to help clients anchor abstract self-functions in concrete thoughts, feelings, and behaviors.
22. Clinicians set limits on a reoccurring basis on the function of self-management therapy and on the roles in therapy.
23. Throughout therapy resolve daily life crises on an "as needed" basis.
24. At a point in the treatment phase when client is able to cope, address PTSD issues identified during diagnosis phase. Treatment should include discussion with client on the approach to take to integrate the traumatic experiences.

Self-Management Phase

25. Clients' self-initiated use, outside of therapy sessions, of psychoeducation information to manage BPD or dual diagnosis characteristics.
26. Clients' self-initiated use of previous homework activity to manage BPD or dual diagnosis characteristics.
27. Clients' self-initiated termination of harmful behaviors, roles, or relationships in their lives.
28. Clients' self-initiated changes in their existing behaviors, roles, and relationships.
29. Clients' self-initiated new behaviors, roles, or relationships in their daily lives.
30. If appropriate, clients stay active or join a relevant self-help or trauma survivors support group such as incest survivors,

TABLE 7.2 Continued

Al-Anon, divorced and separated support group, parents without partners, etc.

Maintenance Phase

31. Episodic therapeutic sessions triggered by an environmental event, a need for a reality check on a specific situation, or to get specific help in self psychological management.
32. If in addiction recovery, clients continue an active recovery program using whatever model of recovery they follow.

purposes this client will have all eight BPD characteristics, resulting in a moderately severe to severe BPD. The client will be female, though it is this clinician's firm belief that "therapist diagnostic discretion" is the major explanation for the extreme sexual imbalance in formally diagnosed borderline clients. The excerpts will be divided into the five phases of therapy noted in Table 7.1. Following each phase will be a commentary highlighting the technical features of self-management therapy within that particular phase of therapy. It is important to reiterate the great individuality in self-management therapy for different borderline clients.

Background Information

Based upon the fact sheet Susan completed, the clinician began the first session knowing the patient was 32 years old, a white female, and never married. She was a salesperson for a computer hardware company. She appeared to be about 5'6" and 100 pounds and her demeanor appeared calm. She avoided eye contact, tending to look down or "beyond" the clinician rather than directly at him. The clinician did not know at this point how Susan had gotten his name or the nature of her presenting problem. The clinician met Susan in the waiting room of his office.

Pre-Diagnosis Phase

C: Hello. You are Susan?
S: (Affirmative head shake, but no verbal reaction.)
C: I'm Dr. Langley. Come with me. (After settling in chairs in

TABLE 7.3 Summary of Self-Management Therapy with Borderline Personality Disorder

Event	Consequence	Intervention
Trauma	idealization and devaluation of	psychoeducation experiment with avoiding
	relationship partner	both states
	reckless impulsiveness	psychoeducation recovery programs behavioral contracts monitor other BPD features
	emotional instability	family of origin relationships psychoeducation on splitting medication
Failed Independence	inappropriate anger	anger management shame education cognitive intervention
	suicidal threats and gestures	behavioral contracts psychoeducation on choice
	self-mutilating behavior	and responsibility hospitalization
Poor self-development	identity diffusion	psychoeducation planned lifestyle changes introspection and journal writing experimenting with new interests
	empty feelings or boredom	psychoeducation reduce isolation increase social activities

TABLE 7.3 Continued

Event	Consequence	Intervention
	frantic efforts to avoid real or imagined abandonment	psychoeducation journal writing
		self-initiated activity monitor other BPD features

his office, the clinician continues speaking.) Before we explore how I might help you, let me tell you that I am a licensed psychologist. I must keep everything we talk about in our sessions confidential. However, there are three exceptions to confidentiality: if you comment about an alleged child abuse incident, or if you make either a homicide or a suicide threat, I am required to report these incidents to public officials as well as to protect you against a suicide attempt or to warn your intended homicide victim. Each therapy session costs $____ and we can help you determine the level of insurance coverage you will have for our sessions. Any questions?

S: No.

C: How might I help you?

S: I don't know where to start. (Begins crying softly and takes a tissue handed to her.) My boyfriend told me he doesn't love me and wants to move out. When I asked him what I had done wrong, he said it wasn't me, but that he needed to get his head on straight. I asked him to come for counseling but he said no. This is not the first time he has done this to me [real or imagined abandonment].

C: How long have you two been together?

S: I've known Pat since we were seniors in college. He dated my best friend our senior year in college. Pat and I started out as drinking buddies. He'd date my girl friend on weekends and he and I would drink together during the week. When we graduated from college we. . . .

C: Who?

S: My girl friend and I. We both got jobs here. Pat kept dating my friend for about the first 6 months we were here, though he lived about 400 miles from here. She developed an interest in another man and then the relationship between Pat and me changed. We became lovers. My girl friend got uncomfortable with the situation, we were roommates, and she moved out. She and I stopped being friends after that. That's really when my problems with Pat began. He didn't come to see me as often as he used to come to see my roommate. In fact, Pat and I began arguing a lot. I remember calling him at night and talking to him for over an hour. Most of the time was spent yelling at each other. I felt like I wasn't important to him. I would accuse him of just being interested in me for sex. I remember the biggest argument we ever had was when I asked him to call me each night while he was in Mexico at his company's annual employee recognition junket. He refused and I got very angry and I did a very dumb thing. I took an overdose of some sleeping and diet pills [inappropriate, intense anger or lack of control of anger].

C: When did this happen?

S: Nine years ago. Fortunately, I drove myself to the emergency room, used a false name, and paid in cash. You are the first person I've ever told about that incident.

C: Any other suicide attempts?

S: My first semester I was away at college. I wasn't going out much socially, I didn't have any close friends: my dad and mom's marriage looked like it was going to end. It was during the first round of academic tests. I was studying hard, getting very little sleep, and missing my home badly. I remember thinking, "It'd just be so easy to go to sleep and never wake up." Next thing I remember my two suitemates had me in the bathroom bent over the toilet and I was vomiting my guts out. I asked them to please keep this situation quiet because if my parents found out, they would remove me from school. As far as I know, my suitemates never told [recurrent suicidal behavior].

C: Have you had any previous psychotherapy?

S: No, except a little in high school.

C: What was the issue?

S: Oh, my mother got on this kick my sophomore year that I

had an eating disorder. It was before such disorders were fashionable. My mother, who is a registered nurse, had been to a conference. I was thin at the time. I was trying to make the gymnastic team.

C: What was your height and weight?

S: I was about 5'5" and weighed about 85 pounds with the biggest hips you've ever seen. My dad used to tease me at the dinner table by suggesting my mother get my hips liposuctioned and reapply it to my chest. I would laugh but that joke always hurt so deeply.

C: Did you do any bingeing and purging during this time? [impulsiveness with alcohol and eating].

S: I only did it for about 3 months before my mother put me in psychotherapy. I was in therapy for about a year. I really liked my therapist. Because of her I stopped the bingeing and purging. Most of my therapy with her was almost social. For awhile she seemed like my mother.

C: Why did the therapy stop?

S: Her husband got transferred. I thought I'd never get over her leaving. I remember deep depressions, raging anger in my room. It got so bad I once took a kitchen knife and cut into pieces two of my favorite "teddy bears" I slept with. I felt so bad. I snuck them out of the house in grocery bags and told my mother I donated them to a Toys for Tot drive at school.

C: Any other therapy?

S: No.

C: So tell me more about you and Pat.

S: Pat does pot, too much I think. I wasn't totally honest with you. In college Pat and I did a lot of pot together. I got bored with it, outgrew it or whatever. I don't know. I used to think it was the pot and booze that bonded Pat and me. I don't do pot anymore and it was just one of many subjects Pat and I argue over. He says our sex life was better when I'd be high. You know, sometimes I wonder if I even love Pat. He has been a part of my life for so long. He's the one who finally forced me to choose a business major in college. Boy, that's another issue we need to get to.

C: What issue is that?

S: My dull boring career in which I make good money [chronic feelings of boredom].

C: You are not sure you even love Pat?

S: In some ways maybe I've outgrown Pat. I want a stable marriage and kids. Sometimes I think Pat graduated from college but didn't leave the mindset. He still parties the way he did 10 years ago. I don't know, maybe Pat is more familiar for me than he is right for me.

C: You seem to have some fundamental questions about Pat's role in your life, or even if there is a role for him in your life.

S: Ah uh.

C: Do you see me helping you sort through these questions?

S: I probably should, but Pat has been such a significant part of my life.

C: If we pursue that issue, we'll do it slowly. Let me ask you what your reaction is so far to this session?

S: I don't know if you can help keep Pat and me together.

C: How would you describe your relationship with your parents?

S: I love my parents dearly. They live about 2 hours from here. I go to see them at least once a month. Mom and I talk two or three times a week. My Daddy is planning on retiring in a year. He and I have your typical father/daughter relationship. He and I never talk. Mom keeps me up with him. My Daddy was wonderful to me while I was growing up. He always pushed me to get good grades and excel in athletics. I remember once in the 5th grade I got a "C" in art. That was not acceptable to Daddy. So I changed the grade to an "A." Of course I got caught but begged my mom not to tell him. She didn't. I admire my Daddy. I wish we were closer [overidealization and devaluation of father].

C: What do you and your mom talk about over the phone?

S: Oh, usually nothing. I tell her how my day went. I may ask her advice on how to handle a situation at work. I hate my job but I love the money. Mom says I may not continue in my career when I get married. Mom talks a lot about Daddy. That's how I keep up with him. Sometimes I even give her advice on how to handle Daddy. We have a great relationship. I don't think a mom and daughter can be too close.

C: Do you and your mom ever disagree?

S: Not anymore. We used to, but since college she and I have grown more and more alike in our views and preferences. I can walk into a clothing store, see a dress, and know instantly it would look good on my mother. Often I'll buy it and send it to her as a surprise. The next time I go home she'll wear it to church and just like I said, she'll look just right in it.

C: Do you and your father ever do anything together?

S: You have to understand my father. He always desperately wanted a son. I was all he got. I've never felt adequate around my father. He loves me, I know. But I know he's disappointed he never had a son. I feel sorry for him. Imagine if you had wanted a son so badly and just couldn't have one. I'm not sure, but I think a lot of my parents marital problems when I was growing up were on that subject. I remember as a little girl, lying in bed and hearing my parents arguing in their bedroom. I once asked Mom if Daddy was mad because I wasn't a little boy. I used to pray that God would make me a boy. I think that's why I excelled so hard at sports as a teenager. But it never seemed to be enough for my Daddy.

C: What's the most traumatic thing you remember happening to you while growing up?

S: In the fifth or sixth grade my father got transferred. We moved from a small town of about 5,000 to a city with over 100,000 people. You know, in some ways I don't think I ever recovered from that move. I lost all my friends. I felt like my safe comfortable place in the universe was canceled. I never had a close friend in junior or senior high school. I sort of seemed to drift without a tether. It was after the move that my parents' marriage problems got worse. I think I got quiet, became a serious student, and really worked to excel in sports. Looking back it seems rather minor. I mean, how many kids move and don't give it a second thought. Imagine if I had been in a military family [initial signs of identity diffusion].

C: Still, that move shook up your world as you knew it and what you lost was permanent, wasn't it?

S: Yes, it was.

C: Furthermore, Susan, I get the sense that with the move you began emphasizing a pattern of living intended to get other people's approval rather than living your own preferences.

S: Hmmm. I hadn't thought of that before. What have I done to myself?

C: I'm not sure you did anything to yourself. I suspect you were a kid coping the very best that you could. Let me ask you, Susan, to give me your reaction to our session so far.

S: I think I need therapy.

C: Do you have any reaction to me?

S: You are easy to talk to. You've shown me a point of view I hadn't thought of. I've always had trouble sharing my feelings with men. Pat was the exception. Now I'm wondering without the pot and booze, maybe he isn't an exception either (tears) [marked shift in her emotions].

Commentary

The preceding hypothetical therapy excerpt may have taken only 20–25 minutes but at this point, the clinician has sufficient documented examples to warrant a likely diagnosis of BPD. In fact, Susan documented all eight BPD characteristics in the DSM-III-R (1987, p. 347). In this instance I would extend the pre-diagnosis phase of therapy into the early part of the second session for the following reasons.

Susan came to therapy wanting to be rescued from Pat or wanting Pat "fixed." Getting the therapy to focus on her can be done via a homework assignment, which I'll describe shortly. Susan may be surprised and shamed if therapy is focused on her through an individual diagnosis. Plus, it is not clear how much her previous therapy addressed or avoided BPD issues, especially the naming of such issues. In addition, the male/female therapeutic relationship clearly calls for a slow transition to the diagnostic phase of therapy. Susan's homework will be straightforward.

C: Susan, your initial request for help was to get you and Pat back in relationship synchrony. As I listened to you, I became aware of some issues that are hampering you as an individual. I have a proposal to make to you. How would you feel if we initially focus therapy on you and then focus on your relationship with Pat?

S: OK.

C: What I'd like you to do is think about it. Would you like for us to meet again?

S: Yes.

C: Between now and our next session, see if you would be ready for me to give you a psychological description of yourself, complete with a diagnosis, that increases your understanding of some themes that go between you and Pat and you and your dad and mom. Do you have any questions of me?

S: Not now.

C: Let's schedule for next week.

The pre-diagnosis phase will end early in the next session if Susan's homework is successful. If not, the pre-diagnosis session will continue until such time that the diagnosis can be communicated to her. Note that therapy can continue into the diagnosis phase of treatment even though the pre-diagnosis phase is not completed. If Susan's homework is not successful, the situation will be ripe for introducing the concept of shame into the therapeutic process. Notice that the beginning of PTSD assessment started in the first session and pertained to the family's move when Susan was in the fifth or sixth grade. This sequencing is possible if the client does not come to the first therapy session in severe or chaotic crisis. Otherwise PTSD assessment is deferred to the diagnostic phase of therapy.

Susan appears on time for her second appointment. She and the clinician exchange pleasantries and take seats.

C: Good to see you again! Well, you had some homework to do. How did it go?

S: I told Pat you don't think he is the problem and you want to focus on me.

C: You seem angry. Are you angry at me?

S: How would you feel if you came to therapy to save a relationship and were told you're the problem.

C: What I said about focusing therapy on you last time left you feeling inadequate or flawed, huh?

S: Can you blame me?

C: Not at all. My comments shamed you. You rightfully are protecting yourself from more shame by using a self protection barrier of anger. Shame will be a subject both of us will discuss a lot during our therapeutic relationship. I'm really curious to hear how your homework went.

S: (Tears.) I don't know why you had to blame me to suggest I do individual therapy.

C: It would be nice if I didn't come with such a high price tag, wouldn't it?

S: (Tears stop.) What do you mean?

C: Here you stumble on a good-sounding therapist, who is easy to talk to and who might be able to help you. Yet, the first session isn't even over and he is shaming you the way so many others have.

S: (Slight smile and affirmative head shake.)

C: Do you know you uncannily match a specific psychiatric diagnosis?

S: Now you are going to tell me I'm crazy?

C: Au contraire! You just have a personality disorder. It even has a name if you are interested.

S: What?

C: Borderline personality disorder.

S: You mean borderline crazy? (said with humor).

C: Look, we need to get something straight. Even when you use humor, I'm not comfortable with your self-put downs. You are in therapy because you have a significant personality disorder. I think our therapy will improve your self-management of this disorder. A major feature of your disorder is a shaky and poor self image. People who have a borderline personality disorder, or BPD, frequently have chaotic lives, tension-filled relationships, and poorly developed self-images. They tend to be very self-destructive and they often struggle against addictive behaviors. They live in near constant fear of being left or abandoned and have quick mood swings. In short, people with BPD are not happy campers, usually because in their heart of hearts they know they are not realizing their potential but don't see a way out.

Commentary

At this point the pre-diagnosis phase comes to an end and the diagnosis phase has begun. The diagnosis phase should follow the steps outlined in Table 7.2 unless Susan develops a crisis. In that no crisis is impacting therapy and because of Susan's cognitive strengths, the clinician, perhaps 20–25 minutes into the second session, moves therapy into the diagnosis phase.

Diagnosis Phase

S: So you say bringing Pat into couples counseling is something we will do down the road.
C: Yes, if that continues to be your preference. Your ability to cope in your relationship with Pat should improve significantly as you develop an understanding of the impact your personality disorder has on that relationship. First, however, is for you to begin to realize what having a borderline disorder requires you to struggle with on a daily basis.

Commentary

If there is no denial nor resistance by the client about the diagnosis, therapy moves to shame issues associated with the BPD label. I have seen shame reactions in clients toward the BPD label who assert they had not heard of the term "borderline" or even now are not sure what it means. As one client said, "It just sounds like it is on the edge. Not a good thing or a good place to be."

C: Susan, let me ask you a question. When you hear the term "borderline personality disorder" how do you feel?
S: (Pause.) The first word that comes to my mind is "yucky." I feel bad inside.
C: Like inadequate, insignificant, inferior, or flawed?
S: Probably not inferior, but certainly the other ones.

C: The feeling primarily associated with each of those psychological conditions is shame. Based upon what you told me about yourself during our first session, can you remember any time in your home when you had a similar feeling?

S: No.

C: How about your father's cruel joke at the dinner table about liposuction for you?

S: Oh, that. Well, maybe.

C: An important part of our therapy will be to reconstruct your shame map of experiences and to help you recognize and manage shame experiences in your future.

Commentary

At this point the clinician would ask the client again about the types of traumatic experiences that may have happened during the first 2 decades or so of her life. As Susan could not remember, or did not report, any additional traumatic events, the therapy was ready to move into the treatment phase.

Treatment Phase

C: There are numerous issues we could address. I don't want your therapy overwhelming you. Let's prioritize. Where do you think your therapy should begin?

S: I'm not sure.

C: I have an idea. Clearly, your relationship with Pat is an important and painful issue for you. Rather than focusing on you and Pat, let's focus on your abandonment issues, fear of being alone, or fear of rejection issue.

S: But there seems so much there.

C: Specifically, then, let's look at the question, "Have you confused love and dependency with Pat?" Do you love Pat?

S: I think I do, but I'm beginning to get confused about that.

C: Are you dependent on Pat?

S: Yes.

C: How do you think that dependency happened?

S: We have been together for so long.

C: Are you suggesting you have trouble separating from people who are close to you?

S: I'm not sure what you mean.

C: What I'm going to say may seem like a stretch to you and, if so, I'll be glad to repeat it. I've heard a common thread in your relationship with Pat and your relationship with both your mom and your dad. That common thread is a clinging dependency. Think of yourself (therapist smiles) as a barnacle clinging to the side of the Queen Mary.

S: That's not a very appealing visual.

C: I think you see yourself as not very appealing. Let me put your "clinging dependency" in a context that I hope will leave you feeling not blamed. Though your father loves you, I think he abandoned you emotionally years ago.

S: (Crying softly.) He supported me in my activities.

C: Yes, activities you pursued, in part, to try to make up for an act of biology with which you had nothing to do. Susan, you split off your awareness of your father's abandonment of you because you were feminine. Rather, you've engaged in compensatory achievement over the years with your father that left you very dependent on his approval and very unsure if he even loves you. Now apply that same scenario to you and Pat.

S: (She and the clinician sit silently for 3–4 minutes while she processes what she just heard.)

C: Can I go on?

S: Sure.

C: Would you be willing to cut down the number of telephone calls between you and your mother?

S: My mother is my best friend. She looks forward to my calls.

C: The reason I ask is there are some amazing similarities in your relationship with your mom that seem to be in your relationship with Pat.

S: Like what?

C: Your dependency on another person that seems to have damaged your independence and self-competence. In both relationships you have merged love and dependency in such a way that you are afraid to be independent. I suspect under the fear of independence is a strong sense of shame associated with believing that you are inadequate, not enough, or in some way fundamentally flawed. For whatever reason, you seem afraid to be independent.

S: I don't want to hear anymore.

C: This may be a good place to stop. Let me ask you, would you consider taking on three pieces of homework?

S: What?

C: Read this brief paper on "splitting." Because you split so often, I want you to read about yourself. Second, would you be willing to reduce your phone calls to your mother to once a week and tell her it is a part of your therapy? Third, think what you'd be willing to say to your father about the relationship the two of you have.

S: I'm not sure about the phone calls to my mom.

C: Ok. Let's play it by ear. Before you leave tell me your reaction to this session.

S: I feel overwhelmed. I feel sad. I'm angry at you but I'm not sure why. I've thought about not coming back.

C: We'll slow down next session. At that time I also want to talk with you about possible medication during therapy.

Commentary

The question of psychotropic medication for borderline clients is really an ongoing question. While clients may begin therapy taking no medication, the stresses of life events or the reduced use of borderline-related coping processes may bring on the need for medication during therapy, most likely an anti-depressant or an anti-anxiety drug. This subject is one the clinician should bring up if the client reports an unremitting sense of being overwhelmed. At this point Susan does not seem to need medication.

The preceding dialogue shows the use of both psychoeducation and homework activities in self-management therapy. The structure of therapy with Susan would continue to dissolve the split in her father-mother perceptions by increasing her differentiation and separation from her mother while building more emotional bonds between Susan and her father. In the pre-diagnosis session Susan revealed all eight BPD characteristics listed in DSM-III-R. Eventually, self-management therapy must address each of these characteristics. With Susan's history of an eating disorder and her current height and weight, the possible continued existence of an eating disorder must be explored. Susan's largely unlabeled and unrecognized shame dynamics will have to be brought to her attention and labelled.

Following the emphasis on Susan's family relationships, her relationship with Pat probably would be the next focus of therapy. It is likely that homework in this area would have a heavy emotional emphasis as a major goal would be to bridge the cognitive/emotional split in Susan.

The therapy phase is likely to last in the 12- to 18-month range. Though skilled in her job, she may be misplaced in her career, or her boredom complaint may be misdirected from another part of her life. She is quite high functioning in her daily life so it is not clear how much she will be willing or need to change. For purposes of this demonstration we will assume Susan limited her therapeutic changes mainly to her private life.

Self-Management Phase

C: Let's see, Susan. We took last week off to celebrate 13 successful months in therapy [during which time she began dating Bob]. If memory serves me right, you had two pieces of homework. One, you were going to see if you could recognized an instance when you used defensive splitting. Two, you were going to see if you recognize when you felt shame or some variant of it.

S: Well, I don't know how well I . . .

C: Let me interrupt you with my own reality check. Are you being honest when you question your own ability to evaluate your behavior, or are you simply hedging against the fact that I may not be pleased?

S: You're confusing me.

C: I'm challenging your unwillingness to credit yourself in an interpersonal situation with me lest I not agree with you, which, I assume then would be real embarrassing, perhaps humiliating to you.

S: Perhaps so. I still say you make mountains out of molehills.

C: I suspect you are right on target. Now how do you think you really did with your homework?

S: Actually, I probably did . . . make that, I did good. In fact it was the same incident where I accomplished both pieces of my homework. I was talking on the phone Sunday night with my mother. In the background I could hear my father tell my mother to tell me hello. I said, "Oh, let me speak to him." My mother said, "He's really wrapped-up right now in his ball game on TV." I said, "OK. Maybe I'll talk with him next time." At first I felt dumb for bothering Daddy. Then I felt hurt about 10 minutes after I got off the phone. This is the reason I said I didn't know how well I did my homework. I split off my feelings of feeling in Daddy's way until about 10 minutes after the end of the phone call.

C: Apparently your mother's comment about your dad's priority of TV over you, and your mother's refusal to call him to the phone, triggered a shame reaction in you that you split off until you were finished dealing with your mother.

S: I guess so.

C: Let me ask you this, then. Who shamed you during that phone call?

S: Until you asked me, it was obvious to me that it was Daddy. Now it's even more obvious to me that it was my mother.

C: I suspect this incident would fit into a long pattern of incidents between you and your mom about your dad. Let me tell you why I think you did so well in your homework. It took you less than 15 minutes to break through the denial that is an essential part of a shame experience and identify your shame experience for what it was. I think you missed that your mother was the real source of your shame in this incident but recognizing the shame trigger wasn't a part of your homework. I think you are trying to be perfect or to hold yourself to a standard that is higher than "good enough."

S: Perhaps.

Commentary

The type of homework described here has as one of its goals client empowerment. It is for this reason that the seemingly innocuous self-questioning by the client is challenged.

With borderline clients these comments usually are not innocuous. Accepting self-credit is the last, but very important, loop in behavior intended to enhance self-efficacy and self-confidence. Susan's confusion is what stimulated her shame. Believing it was her father, when it really was her mother, suggests some ongoing enmeshment between her and her mother and some ongoing emotional distance between her and her father. When hearing or seeing such distorted perceptions, clinicians must ask if their clients are functioning "good enough" in the circumstances. The client's preference for higher levels of functioning would be reason enough to continue therapy. Otherwise, homework performance at the level Susan achieved would be one indicator for moving Susan's therapy to the maintenance phase. One additional vignette in Susan's therapy provides additional support for moving her therapy to the next phase.

C: We ended last session talking about your relationship with Bob. I had raised the question if your "clinging dependency" was creating problems in this relationship. You agreed to think about it. What did you come up with?

S: I'm very proud of what I came up with. I am no longer dating Bob. I never figured out if I was clinging or what. I did decide that I shouldn't have to work so hard in a relationship and constantly not know where I stood. I did recognize that with Bob I was living on the edge of being abandoned. When I did recognize that condition, that's when I knew it was time to get out of Dodge.

C: How did you end the relationship?

Commentary

Terminating a harmful or unfulfilling relationship is a highly positive sign that a borderline client's therapy has been "good enough." The self-efficacy and self-initiation required in such behavior reflects the type of growth that is a major thrust of self-management therapy.

It is important in making the transition from the self-management phase to the maintenance phase that careful attention be given to abandonment issues. Therapy is not at an end.

Rather, the client is taking over full self-management of her/ his therapy. Clients are told they can make appointments any time on an "as needed" basis. There does not have to be an emergency to warrant an appointment. An occasional phone call to the therapist may provide sufficient reorientation.

Susan called for an appointment about 8 months after her session in which she described her break up with Bob. The clinician did not know the purpose of the session.

Maintenance Phase

C: So very good to see you again, Susan. To what do I owe the pleasure of this meeting?

S: I've been doing really well. My father died a month ago yesterday.

C: Susan, I am so sorry to hear that.

S: It was quite a shock. He died of a massive heart attack. Even though it has been 8 months since I've seen you, I wanted to check a couple of things with you. Mom is having difficulty dealing with Daddy's death. She talked with me last week about selling the house and moving here to be closer to me. I kept my cool with her but I'm freaking out inside. Do you think it's a good idea for my mother and me to live in the same town?

C: Why don't you answer your own question and let's talk about your answer.

S: I think it's what Mom wants to do and I don't think it's good for me.

C: I've got to compliment you on your integrated answer and how you avoided splitting those two contradictory states.

S: I've worked so hard to get what independence from Mother I do have. I think I would lose all I have gained if she and I lived in the same town.

C: You aren't sure your boundaries are strong enough to keep your mother at bay?

S: True. So I need some help. What should I do?

C: What is your preference as to where your mother lives?

S: I think, I mean, I want her to stay where she is.

C: Why?

S: Because I can handle her at this distance.

C: Let me add to your point. We always hear not to make major decisions in the immediate aftermath of a major death in our lives. Perhaps with the help of your family attorney your mom could be counseled to give herself at least a year to let her new life evolve. Don't sell the house at this time. Stay there for a year and then have your mom look at her options.

S: That certainly makes financial sense.

C: Remember, more importantly, it's your preference. Clearly, then, during this year you have to address the possible issue of you and your mom living in the same city.

S: That task just seems overwhelming right now. But, you are right. I have the better part of a year to deal with Mother on that subject.

C: Remember, you don't have to approach this issue alone, Susan. More individual therapy or even some mother/daughter work could be very helpful to you.

S: This has been very helpful in getting me refocused.

C: I'm here should we need to go any further down this path.

Commentary

The availability of the clinician in the maintenance phase is a crucial part of self-management therapy. While such sessions may seldom be used by borderline clients, this availability can provide a front line defense against a life circumstance escalating to a life crisis. Very often such sessions can be handled in a 5-minute phone call. In fact, if the phone call takes much more than 5 minutes, a face-to-face session is probably warranted. As noted in the preceding dialogue, the sessions are very task-focused and problem-solving in nature. While psychoeducation is used liberally, the client's problem is taken at face value and a solution crafted. It is important that each maintenance session end with clinicians communicating their availability. It is not unusual for maintenance sessions to reactivate the therapy phase. It is important to remember that BPD is not cured, it is simply better managed. It is reasonable to expect that as borderline clients observe their improved self-management skills and see the benefits they derive, they would want to improve these skills. This perspective is a viable alternative to the traditional therapy experience with borderline clients where there are many premature stops to therapy.

REFERENCES

American Psychiatric Association. (1987). *Diagnostic and Statistical Manual of Mental Disorders* (3rd edition-revised). Washington, DC: Author.

Bandura, A. (1971). Self-efficacy: Toward a unifying theory of behavioral change. *Psychological Review, 84*(2), 191–215.

Swartz, M., Blazer, D., George, L., & Winfield, I. (1990). Estimating the prevalence of borderline personality disorder in the community. *Journal of Personality Disorders, 4*(3), 257–272.

Widiger, T. A., & Rogers, J. H. (1989). Prevalence and comorbidity of personality disorders. *Psychiatric Annals, 19*(3), 132–136.

Iatrogenic Factors That May Disrupt Therapy 8

The psychiatric dictionary defines "iatrogeny" as the "production or inducement of any harmful change in the somatic or psychic condition of a patient by means of the words or actions of the doctor [clinician]" (Hinsie & Campbell, 1975, p. 371). The iatrogenic factors referred to in this chapter pertain to all activities associated with the processes in psychotherapy. For example, a secretary may tell a borderline client that the clinician is not taking phone calls but not know that the clinician told the client to call during office hours if there was a need to talk. This would be an iatrogenic factor in that client's therapy.

This chapter will challenge what seems to be an axiom in both the psychotherapy literature and in professional clinical communities: It is psychogenic (origination within the mind or psyche) factors within borderline individuals that make them such difficult clients (Hinsie & Campbell, 1975, p. 613). This psychogenic interpretation by clinicians of their experiences with borderline clients began with psychoanalysts in the 1930s and seems to have been adopted by every mental health discipline from professional counselors, addiction counselors, social workers, and psychologists, to all schools of psychiatry. It only takes a cursory review of the literature, or a short encounter with a colleague at a professional convention, to realize the hold that this psychogenic interpreta-

185

tion has on clinicians and on professional clinical communities. To prove the point, I frequently tell groups of mental health clinicians that if they want an instant bonding experience, stand up and announce to a group of their colleagues that they currently have ten borderline clients in their therapy caseload. The outpouring of knowing looks, gallows humor, and the identification with the "poor" clinician that follows should reaffirm the near unanimity of the sociogenic or institutional prejudice against borderline clients.

For example, if the previously alluded-to borderline client, who was blocked by the secretary from talking with the clinician, hangs up the phone and cuts him or herself with a razor blade, it is highly unlikely the major cause of the cutting incident will be seen as a poorly run office or inadequate communication by the clinician with his support staff. The explanation of the self-cutting behavior is much more likely to be psychogenic, based on a well-known feature (e.g., poor impulse control, low frustration tolerance, excessive clinging dependency on the clinician) of BPD. This chapter will make the case to professional clinicians to consider non-psychogenic reasons why some borderline clients demand extra time and energy from clinicians. The current plethora of psychogenic explanations for why borderline clients are so difficult all carry heavy overtones of blaming-the-victim.

In no way am I suggesting that borderline clients are not difficult clients on occasion. Rather, my objective in this chapter is to raise three questions for professional mental health clinicians to consider. First, for a category of clients who, according to the DSM-III-R, can be categorized as "borderline" based upon 56 different combinations of diagnostic features, does it not stretch credulity to consider this entire heterogeneous category of clients as difficult in therapy? Second, from the perspective of who wields the most power in a psychotherapy relationship, especially in the early phases of therapy, might there not be forces operating other than psychogenic forces within borderline clients that could disrupt or make for tumultuous therapy? Third, is there not a disturbing parallel between clinicians' labeling borderline clients as difficult due to client characteristics and our culture's now discredited explanations that so many blacks are poor because of their characteristics (e.g., lazy, shiftless, untrustworthy, etc.) or so few women hold positions of political or economic leadership because of their characteristics (e.g., caregivers, mentally soft, pushovers in an argument, etc.)?

It is important to warn against two outcomes from reading this chapter. First, I in no way want to idealize borderline clients as the hapless victims of the clinician class. There clearly are some borderline clients who are difficult clients and who are committed to disrupting their therapy, and maybe even victimizing the therapist. It is important to remember that at any point in time, however, it is unlikely that most people in the United States with BPD are in therapy; in fact, most have not been diagnosed as having BPD. So, perhaps, there may be an iatrogenic factor or two operating within the diagnosing and treating activities of people with BPD that is making them "difficult clients." It is also important to remember that many of these "difficult borderline clients" in outpatient therapy leave their sessions and continue their lives as professionals, spouses, parents, students, and in other productive roles.

Second, it would be quite counterproductive simply to change the blame game from blaming borderline clients for being "difficult" to blaming their clinicians for being "non-empathic," "abusive," or "incompetent." To avoid such dichotomous thinking or splitting, it may be helpful to draw a connection between the limits in the psychoanalytic framework and the psychogenic explanations of borderline clients as "difficult." Furthermore, the sociogenic solidarity within professional clinician communities as to the image of borderline clients seems a direct result of the hegemony in BPD theories held by psychoanalysis until the 1980s.

As noted in Chapter 4, psychoanalytic theory has no social psychological dimension to it. All psychoanalytic explanations must be psychogenic. That is, all psychoanalytic explanations must be intrapsychic. For example, if borderline clients resume cutting themselves when their therapist goes on vacation, the explanation for the self-mutilating behavior may be related to the lack of object constancy or the absence of evocative memory on the part of the clients. If therapists express anger at their borderline clients for making some request, the explanation used for the therapists' behavior likely will be based on countertransference. Note that object constancy, evocative memory, and countertransference explanations are each psychogenic in nature.

Left unexplored in the above examples are possible iatrogenic factors to explain what is going on between the client and therapist. For example, many clinicians will take emergency phone calls during a session, yet not allow clients to make emergency phone calls to the clinician at home. This differential in prerogative and value placed on client and clinician time seems much more an iatrogenic factor in the client-clinician relationship than it does an intrapsychic issue for either of the participants.

To extend this line of thinking, virtually all psychotherapy with borderline clients occurs within a community of clinicians. Perhaps the most compelling evidence of this sociogenic (produced by or formed from a social aggregate) influence on borderline clients' psychotherapy is the reputation and explanation attached to their tendency to terminate therapy prematurely and/or disruptively. There is a near universal belief in the various professional communities that part of borderline clients "difficultness" is their tendency to stop therapy unilaterally. Granted, the clear trend in psychotherapy research with these clients supports the belief that they drop out of therapy in disproportionate numbers. However, it is important to keep two factors in mind. First, few other psychiatric disorders, and perhaps none, report average length of therapy running 5 to 7 years. Second, psychoanalytic-infused therapy is simply an inappropriate therapy for BPD. This type of therapy encourages dropping out by borderline clients. It is interesting that Linehan and Heard (1992, pp. 264–265) reported an 83% retention rate with borderline clients after 1 year of behavior therapy.

It should be noted that psychoanalytic theory has no sociogenic or sociological dimension associated with it. In psychoanalytic thought "psychogenic" and "iatrogenic" are merged into a psychogenic perspective. Psychoanalytic thought simply ignores the sociogenic influence that clinicians' professional communities have on clinicians' and borderline clients' psychotherapy experiences. The social beliefs about BPD held in the professional clinician communities of which I am aware, are shaped primarily by psychoanalytic tenets.

The second dominant social influence on clinicians seems to be their *negative* clinical experiences with borderline clients. I could find no research or even commentary on the following question: How widespread is the practice of diagnosing BPD on a post hoc basis after there has been a premature termination or a serious disruption in the therapy process? My informal surveys and conversations at professional meetings suggest that the practice of "diagnosis by disruption" may be quite widespread. A Kohutian clinician would have no trouble justifying this practice for an individual clinical case. However, the widespread prejudice and discrimination that seems to have emanated from this practice raises a serious ethical question regarding fairness of treatment of borderline clients by professional clinician communities.

The practice of diagnosing BPD via "therapy disruption" may contribute to a self-fulfilling prophecy among clinicians. BPD may be avoided consciously as a diagnosis for non-disruptive clients. Because of the nature of BPD, there is almost always an axis I diagnostic option such as depression, anxiety, addiction, etc. The social prejudice against BPD is so strong in professional clinician communities, I have heard respected clinicians admit to avoiding making a BPD diagnosis when "another one will do."

A second unintended consequence of diagnosing by disruption is legitimately to miss a BPD diagnosis with a compliant borderline client. With this group of clients the undiagnosed BPD becomes the clinician's secret that is withheld from clients so that they don't become offended (possible clinician projection?) or create a self-fulfilling prophecy. I have heard numerous psychologists state that with some borderline clients they withhold sharing the BPD diagnosis with the client and provide a diagnosis based upon one or another BPD features such as depression, addiction, etc.

Given the self-management approach to BPD presented in this book, it seems likely that unidentified and unmanaged shame is a central force that disrupts the therapy of borderline clients. To extend the thinking in this chapter, the shame that sometimes disrupts the therapy of borderline clients has psychogenic, iatrogenic and sociogenic sources.

In a therapeutic relationship with a borderline client, the clinician is exposed to excessive levels of toxic shame. According to the self-management model of BPD, shame is the core emotion of this disorder. However, given the psychoanalytic influence on the conception and therapy of BPD, shame largely has been ignored as a pathological force (Morrison, 1989, p. 5).

Concrete illustrations of how the three sources of shame— psychogenic, iatrogenic, and sociogenic—are activated in and by the clinical relationship may be helpful. Borderline clients have a well-known tendency to merge psychologically with their clinicians. One of the ways this merger occurs is through projective identification (PI). It is through PI that the client's psychogenic source of shame is activated. PI is largely an unconscious process or a process that occurs outside the awareness of the two participants. It is a process that occurs in three steps between two people: (1) one person projects an unwanted feeling onto another person (e.g., "My therapist doesn't respect me" (inadequacy), "My client doesn't seem committed to our therapy" (inadequacy); (2) the other person unknowingly introjects the feeling projected onto him or her (shame in this example) and then thinks, feels and acts the emotion (e.g., "No matter what I say the therapist will think I'm stupid," "The client acts like I can't be trusted"); and (3) the first person takes the unwanted feeling back, but in a revised and more palatable form ("I'm not the only person the clinician doesn't respect," "There aren't many clinicians who would subject themselves to this client's behavior").

Because of the diluted boundaries and partially lost identities that are always a part of both a PI experience and a shame experience, it is very difficult to be aware of these experiences when they are happening. Both sets of experiences involve a compromise in the autonomy of the self. The distortions associated with both PI and shame are more likely to be understood as projection. This tendency for clinicians to interpret PI as projection also encourages them to "bypass" their shame experience. In so doing a psychogenic focus is maintained and the interplay between client and clinician is understood as the dynamics of the client's BPD. While this understanding is a distortion, it is also safe for the clinician. Such an interpretation also is buttressed by the intrapsychic bias of psychoanalytic theory.

There is perhaps no stronger message in this book than recognizing the historical and contemporary denial and minimization of iatrogenic factors on the disruption of psychotherapy with borderline clients. The very genesis of the word "borderline" arose out of therapy-disruptive iatrogenic factors. Borderline clients were not quite able to endure the regressive intensity of psychoanalysis, but neither were they psychotic and, hence, unable to participate. They were borderline, and the clinician had to lighten the therapy approach if the client was to be helped and not harmed. Reading the clinical literature on borderline clients in the 1930s, 1940s and 1950s, it is hard to miss the sense of inadequacy and frustration communicated by the clinician-authors.

In fact, inadequacy-based shame may be at the core of iatrogenic factors that disrupt therapy with borderline clients. I have yet to talk to a clinician who has a therapy approach with BPD that works reliably or in which the clinician has great self confidence. Not all clinicians can be expected to be comfortable and effective with all diagnostic groups. However, I find it remarkable never to have run into a clinician who is comfortable or who prefers to work with BPD. This discomfort, inadequacy, and avoidance certainly can be expected to reverberate within the therapeutic relationship. It should be easy to imagine, especially with the influence of projective identification, the influence of inadequacy spawning shame within the clinical relationship. ("The clinician doesn't care about me or she/he would let me make a phone call when I panic"; "I'm not a bottomless well. The more I give the more this client seems to need.")

There are sound psychological reasons self-management therapy supports a proactive clinician role in working with BPD. The proactive role of the clinician is intended to mitigate the influence of splitting on the therapeutic relationship. Such leadership is to provide a consistent externalized source of self-direction that can be internalized by the client via role modeling. Client passivity and extended silences within therapy sessions hide from the clinician the presence and type of splitting the client might be doing. The clinician's proactive role also provides a boundary setting function for the client to use.

The following is a non-exhaustive list of seven conditions within therapy that can produce iatrogenic-induced disruptions of therapy with borderline clients:

1. Therapy sessions are too emotionally intense for the client due to the intensity of client-clinician interaction or because of the multiplicity of subjects being focused on in therapy.
2. The clinician had not assessed adequately the need to provide the client with guidance and structure in situations where the client has impulse control problems.
3. Clinicians must proactively recognize and titrate their clients' idealization/devaluation cycle toward the clinician.
4. Clinicians explore and try to anticipate the occurrence of abandonment panic in the therapy relationship or in a client's social relationship that therapy may impact.
5. Relapse of addictive behavior leaves little the clinician can do but address the relapse. Each clinician should establish with the client who is addicted what the immediate impact on therapy will be if the client resumes an active addiction or using phase.
6. Self-destructive behaviors, unless they are potentially lethal, should be discussed with the client and alternative forms of behavior sought. If the self-destructive behavior seems to be escalating toward lethal levels, then the clinician must intervene against the client's will.
7. Suicidal gestures and attempts must be responded to but should not significantly disrupt therapy unless iatrogenic factors are behind such behavior.

Examining iatrogenic factors that are disrupting therapy is one of the few times when self-management therapy focuses on the therapeutic relationship. It may provide clinicians with a certain degree of shame immunization in working with BPD to adopt the "good enough" standard detailed in the therapy goals listed in Chapter 6. Given the client's life circumstances, "good enough" will vary in meaning. At least such a standard has, as its advantages, a demonstrable standard for declaring therapy successful and it reduces the open-ended nature so characteristic of therapy with BPD.

Because of the confidential and technical nature of a clinical relationship, clinicians cannot have their clinical self-efficacy or self-worth reaffirmed by significant others in their private lives. This reaffirmation, or at worst release from fault, seems to occur by reading the professional literature on BPD and talking with professional colleagues, where the problems working with BPD are reaffirmed and shame is dissolved through the exchange of borderline client "war stories." The sociogenic reinforcement that clinicians get from their colleagues as to the difficulties in working with BPD may help them bypass the shame they feel as individual clinicians. It certainly may be working as a creative suppressant against the development of new therapeutic approaches for working with BPD.

Additional comments about clinician shame are in order. It is important to remember that Tomkins (1987) and Kaufman (1989) describe shame as an auxiliary emotion. Thus, shame is carried, expressed, or suppressed by another emotion. For clinicians working with BPD, it is likely that anger or fear serve as emotional masks for shame. In interactions with clients, shame is bypassed but the clinician still has an emotional reaction (Lewis, 1971, pp. 196–198). This involves a split emotional reaction in which the shame component is split off and is out of awareness.

The sociogenic source of clinician shame in working with borderline clients may begin with the inadequate psychoanalytic theory of BPD that continues to be accepted within clinician communities. Until the 1980s there were no published theories of BPD that challenged the psychoanalytic model. However, the vast majority of clinicians in the United States were not trained in psychoanalysis. This training inadequacy had two consequences. First, clinicians not trained in psychoanalysis were not qualified to critique what now seem to be obvious inadequacies in the psychoanalytic model of BPD. This gap feeds a tendency within the psychoanalytic literature to refrain from fundamental criticism of the psychoanalytic model. One author may highlight aggression over guilt, while another may acknowledge a role for the father in the development of the child's identity. However, I found no published sources, for example, that even hinted at challenging the core psychoanalytic belief that BPD develops if object constancy fails to occur by year 3 or 4 in a toddler's life. As such, the professional psychoanalytic literature appears very conservative and not particularly tolerant of voices of diversity or dissent. The more dominant sociogenic force among psychoanalytic writers is to try to make psychoanalytic principles and procedures work rather than question and expand, or even replace, traditional psychoanalytic thought.

A second consequence has been the development of "trickle down" or diluted psychoanalysis. Throughout this book the term "psychoanalytic-influenced" theories, techniques, or clinicians has been used. This term refers to non-psychoanalytic trained clinicians having to use psychoanalytic assumptions and concepts when working with borderline clients. Because of the lack of a BPD model independent of psychoanalytic influences, the non-psychoanalytic clinician communities had no choice of an alternative BPD model until the mid-1980s. Rather than devoting resources to developing a new clinical model of BPD, clinician communities en masse seem to have adopted the psychoanalytic assumptions about BPD and then worked with these clients the best they could. Such clinicians were saddled with a double negative. They lacked the training to provide "tailored" psychoanalytic therapy to borderline clients and these clinicians seem to have introjected the psychoanalytic community's negativity, pessimism and doctrinaire attitudes about borderline clients.

The above described technical inadequacy and rejecting attitude among most clinician communities toward borderline clients could be two sources of shame with which clinicians have to cope. Projection is a major coping mechanism for managing shame. In Chapter 3 the psychoanalyst, Leon Wurmser, identified nine different affects used to mask feelings that shut out the sense of shame. To these nine, Helen Brock Lewis added a tenth—humor. The clinician humor that I have heard about borderline clients seems to have as its pri-

mary goal tension or shame reduction. An unavoidable outcome of this humor, however, seems to be the overt disparage-
ment of borderline clients. The actual consequence of the
humor seems to be to redress the felt inadequacies of clinicians in dealing with BPD by reaffirming how impossible borderline clients can be. Perhaps without intending to, clinicians sociogenically are passing their shame onto their
already shame-burdened borderline clients through projective identification.

For those clinicians who may get caught unknowingly in
managing their clinically induced shame through projective
identification (PI), a general description of this process may
help disrupt it. If the objective is to protect the clinician-bor-
derline client relationship, it is insignificant who throws the
first PI stone. As a process in shame management, it is important that clinicians take responsibility for their role in PI. The
condition that can generate shame is any personally significant condition in which clinicians believe they may be insignificant, irrelevant, inept, inadequate, incompetent, or ineffective. Clearly, the psychoanalytic theory and therapy of BPD
is just such a condition under which clinicians work. The general clinical practice has been to assume that the conditions
for shame have been projections from borderline clients.
Rather, the intense shame dynamics so characteristically a
part of many clinical relationships with borderline clients are
perhaps iatrogenically induced by therapy processes guided
by psychoanalytic assumptions.

So the first step in iatrogenically generated shame is the
clinician's knowledge (belief or fear) that the therapeutic processes occurring in therapy with BPD clients really do not
work, or are inadequate. This clinical deficiency, of course,
leaves the clinician in a state of inadequacy or ineptness. Because of the tradition not to question the fundamental inadequacies of the psychoanalytic model of BPD, clinicians project the source of their inadequacy or ineptness onto their
borderline clients. Such projections are easily supported by
the psychoanalytic assumptions that clients with BPD have a
pre-oedipal disorder, use primitive coping mechanisms, seek
symbiosis with their clinicians, etc.

Step two of clinicians handling their therapy-generated

shame probably occurs from an interaction of clinician assumptions and borderline clients' behaviors. These clients act in ways to reinforce clinicians' beliefs about their clinical inadequacy or clinical ineptness. However, many clinicians tend to see such client behaviors as reinforcing the stereotype of clients with BPD as difficult, rather than the clients' behaviors reinforcing the ineptness in the psychoanalytic model of BPD. The reality is that clinicians get caught in therapy-generated forces that can be very shaming and many handle their shame experience by projecting it onto or blaming their clients.

The third step of clinicians' PI is to resign themselves to long-term therapy with the BPD client and not challenge them unduly. Rather, the clinician assumes a role of a clinical "babysitter." Another version of this third step might be to refer the client to another clinician or to try only haphazardly to keep the client in therapy as the client's "no show" rate increases. Certainly, at this point, the clinician would benefit from a consultation. However, finding an experienced colleague not tarnished by the psychoanalytic assumptions about BPD is extremely difficult. As a consequence, many clinicians resort to the aforementioned "borderline humor" with other colleagues as one of the ways to manage their iatrogenically induced shame. Of course, it is important to remember that PI is an interpersonal process. While this description of PI was from the clinician's perspective, the client also has been involved and affected by the PI process.

A more clinically adequate model of BPD should help every clinician who works with borderline clients. However, it is imperative that this model accord shame a central role in both BPD and in the clinician–client relationship. Primary shame is a psychogenic feature of BPD. Secondary shame is a primary iatrogenic factor of the clinical relationship involving clinicians and borderline clients. It appears likely that the failure of a majority of clinicians to recognize and to manage these two sources of shame is the major basis for the sociogenic sources of tertiary shame which seem so pervasive in clinicians' comments to each other about BPD. The sociogenic function of these discussions seems to be to allow one clinician to verify with another that they share a clinical inadequacy experience relative to borderline clients. So, rather than dissolving a clinician's shame, such communication seems to be sharing the shame with another clinician through a repetition of the belief that "all borderline patients are difficult to treat" and, as long as this "fact" is accepted by clinician communities, individual clinicians can bypass their own shame.

The psychoanalytic perspective on shame considers shame primarily an infantile and primitive emotion (Morrison, 1989, p. 5). Such a developmentally phase-specific concept of shame is counter to the experiences of every adult with whom I have had a discussion about shame. Clearly, shame can occur in adult experiences without being a repetition of a primitive emotion that occurred in infancy. An additional problem for adults who knowingly or unknowingly accept the psychoanalytic-influenced concept of shame, is that to have a shame experience is to be reduced to a child. The prevailing idea, promulgated in psychoanalytic thought, that shame is a primitive and infantile emotion ignores the work on shame done by Tomkins, Kaufman, Nathanson, Bradshaw, and several other non-psychoanalytic clinician/authors.

The psychoanalytic viewpoint that emphasizes the major source of shame as the child–caretaker relationship is probably true for children under 5 who do not attend a day school, day-care, go to a babysitter, and who have a full-time at-home mother. This traditional way of growing up now applies to less than 10% of children in the United States. Consequently, with the enormous social changes since World War II, the inadequacies in the psychoanalytic-influenced concept of shame continue to grow. Although no data exist to prove the point, it seems intuitively clear that nonparental sources of shame—peers, secular authority figures, work, bosses, colleagues, service providers in the market place, strangers, ourselves—far outweigh the shame experiences we have with our parents.

Clinicians, then, are left to treat a major personality disorder like BPD with a childhood-based concept of shame. Yet, distorted adult identity, which is largely a function of the interplay between narcissism and shame, is a central dimension of BPD.

Perhaps the self-management model of BPD presented in this book and the central role played by shame will provide clinicians with the framework and techniques needed to address the heretofore latent aspects of shame. At the very least, perhaps the self-management model will raise the consciousness of clinicians regarding their psychogenic, iatrogenic, and sociogenic reactions to borderline clients.

In bringing this book to a close, a few carefully chosen words seem in order on the subject of sex between a clinician and a client. I could find no published data on the diagnostic categories of clients who become involved sexually with their clients. Because of their self disorder, borderline clients are at risk to become sexually involved with their clinicians. The subject of sex between clinician and client will grow in importance over the next decade as states move to make such activity a felony criminal offense for clinicians.

The professional literature notwithstanding, many borderline clients do not express themselves disruptively or violently in therapy. They may express themselves seductively or sexually. One of the rationales for titrating the intensity of therapy is to help borderline clients contain their emotions. With weak self functions it is easy for these clients to move from feeling intense, to feeling passionate, to feeling sexual. The flooding or contaminating of different feelings or the mislabeling of feelings (dependency often can be confused with intimacy), is an all too frequent experience of borderline clients. The sexualization or the abrupt disruption of a therapy relationship are simply two manifestations of a more general relationship problem facing individuals with BPD. Poor self boundaries create considerable interpersonal pressure that threaten the integrity and purpose of a relationship. A worker with a BPD, who idealizes the boss, shares personal information with this superior. The boss, feeling compassionate or sorry for the worker, offers some advice. The worker via projective identification, now believes the boss considers him/her special. With this seemingly innocent crossing of relationship boundaries, a dynamic is set in motion between these two people that can generate shame scenarios.

It seems to be in the nature of BPD that great interpersonal pressure is often a part of the interaction with borderline individuals. It is possible that the interpersonal basis of loneliness or emptiness reported by so many individuals with BPD may reflect their experiences of having individuals back away from them because of the pressure on the ego and the self that so often exists. Clinicians usually do not have the option of backing off from this interpersonal pressure. Because of borderline clients' weak selves, this interpersonal pressure, if not understood and titrated properly by the clinician, can lead either to a merger experience, with the danger of the relationship becoming sexualized, or to a distancing or abandoning experience with the danger of the relationship becoming violent or being terminated by the client. In either instance, shame is operating to distort the clinical relationship. It takes real skill and persistence on the part of the clinician to manage this split within the client's self and interpersonal style, to assess if there is projective identification going on between the clinician and client, and to monitor whatever sexual feelings the clinician has developed for the client or the client for the clinician.

It is important to remember that therapy with a borderline client usually lasts for a long time. Softened boundaries between clinician and client are virtually inevitable over this extended length of time. It is important for clinicians to recognize when significant levels of sexual feelings develop toward a client. It is important that a clinician act on these feelings immediately by seeking a supervisory session or by talking about these feelings with a trusted colleague. Handling such feelings in isolation or in secrecy is solid evidence of the shame associated with such feelings. It is because of the presence of shame and the danger of denying its presence by "acting through it" that clinicians should seek preventative consultation.

James Masterson, in an article written for *Self* magazine in September 1989, referred to BPD as the disorder of the 90s. While he did not provide a sociological analysis for why this disorder may reflect the times, there are some interesting possibilities. Many institutions are splitting from within. Families are split by divorce. Schools are split by class, race, funding resources, and polarized philosophies of education. Churches are split by strife over moderate versus fundamentalist interpretation of doctrine. Businesses are paralyzed or split in their profit mission by the short half-life of technology, the loss of employee loyalty, and the added stress and lowered morale occurring from downsizing. If the model of BPD presented in this book is accurate, the macro-social trends mentioned here will increase the prevalence of BPD. While not negating the psychoanalytic model of BPD, the self-management model will support causative factors far larger than child-caregiver interactions. As splitting is inherent in BPD and seems to arise out of inadequate mirroring or idealizing, or out of incomplete autonomy, or non-reinforced autonomy or as a result of a traumatic experience, so may BPD be an unavoidable consequence of a pluralistic post-industrial society. The level of social cohesion may mirror the level of self cohesion in individuals. As more research attention continues to focus on BPD, our epidemiological and clinical management knowledge will continue to grow, along with our knowledge of what causes BPD.

REFERENCES

Hinsie, L. E., & Campbell, R. J. (1975). *Psychiatric dictionary* (4th ed.). New York: Oxford University Press.

Kaufman, G. (1989). *The psychology of shame.* New York: Springer Publishing Co.

Lewis, H. B. (1971). *Shame and guilt in neurosis.* New York: International Universities Press.

Linehan, M. M., & Heard, H. L. (1992). Dialectical behavior therapy for borderline personality disorder. In J. C. Clarkin, E. Marziali, & H. Monroe-Blum (Eds.), *Borderline personality disorder: Clinical and empirical perspectives* (pp. 248–267). New York: The Guilford Press.

Morrison, A. P. (1989). *Shame: The underside of narcissism.* Hillsdale, NJ: The Analytic Press.

Tomkins, S. S. (1987). Shame. In D. L. Nathanson (Ed.), *The many faces of shame.* New York: The Guilford Press.

Index